GW00858604

BLACKBIRD

COLD WAR SPYPLANES

STEVE STONE

FOREWORD

In April 1986, following an attack on American soldiers in a Berlin disco, President Reagan ordered the bombing of Muammar Qaddafi's terrorist camps in Libya. This was in response to the 1986 Berlin discotheque bombing. The bombing had killed three people and around 230 injured when a bomb placed under a table near the disk jockey's booth of the La Belle discothèque. The bomb exploded at 1:45 am. After the bombing raid in Libya - 40 Libyan casualties were reported along with one US plane, which was shot down, resulting in the death of two airmen. An SR-71 was to fly over Libya and take photos recording the damage the F-111's had inflicted after the raid on Libya. Qaddafi had established a 'line of death', a territorial marking across the Gulf of Sidra, swearing to shoot down any intruder that crossed the boundary. The only aircraft that had a chance of beating theses defences was the SR-71 and it would be its ability to fly faster than any other aircraft and outrun the pursuing missiles before they ran out of fuel. This is a narrative from an SR-71 Blackbird pilot sent to photograph the aftermath of the bombing raid on Libya. Based at Beale Air Force Base in California, detachments of the SR-71 flew from Mildenhall in the east of England and from Kadena on the Japanese island of Okinawa.

'On the morning of April 15, our SR-71 rocketed past the line at 2,125 mph. I was piloting the SR-71 spy plane, being accompanied by Maj Walter Watson, the aircraft's RSO (Reconnaissance Systems Officer. We had crossed into Libya and were approaching our final turn over the bleak desert landscape, when Walter informed me that he was receiving missile launch signals. I quickly increased our speed, calculating the time it would take for the weapons-most likely SA-2 and SA-4 surface-to-air missiles capable of Mach 5 - to reach our altitude. I estimated that we could beat the rocket-powered missiles to the turn and stayed our course, betting our lives on the plane's performance. Some way behind the missiles attempted to catch us, but even at Mach 5 they ran out of fuel before they had a chance to even get close. After several extremely long seconds, we made the turn and blasted toward the Mediterranean 'You might want to pull it back,' Walter suggested. It was then that I noticed I still had the throttles full forward. The plane was flying a mile every

1.6 seconds, well above our Mach 3.2 limit. It was the fastest we would ever fly. I pulled the throttles to idle just south of Sicily, but we still managed to fly past the refuelling tanker awaiting us over Gibraltar."

***

The spy planes of the 1950s were all aircraft way ahead of their time. The first, the U-2 is still in service today over 50 years after its first flight. This alone is testament to the design and engineering - that a replacement is not felt needed, partly due to satellite surveillance and partly due to the cost of developing a new manned spy plane, with so many different drone surveillance aircraft on drawing boards and being introduced. The U-2 has been and still is flying over countries of interest, collecting intelligence more recently the war on terror. It will continue to fly, even though retirement is on the cards. Although, due to a technology gap the retirement date has yet to be agreed.

As for the SR-71 Blackbird and A-12, they are still the fastest jet powered plane ever to fly. Only the rocket-powered North American X-15 flew faster. It still holds the official world record for the highest speed ever reached by a manned aircraft of Mach 6.72. Compared to the SR-71 with a top speed of Mach 3.3 and slightly faster A-12 with Mach 3.35. The top speed was limited by the engine temperature as the speed limit was nothing to do with the aircraft, it was to do with the engines. Right in front of the engines was a temperature probe. When that temperature was around 427C (800F) that's as fast as they were allowed to go. The makers of the engine - Pratt & Whitney - would not warranty or guarantee anything beyond 427. After that, the engine could come unglued or you could shed turbine blades. The fuel used to power the A-12 and SR-71 could extinguish cigarettes due to its very high flashpoint. The story goes that when they were building the planes, Kelly Johnson, the designer realised the external temperatures would get over 300C (600F), all the leading edges 300C and the rest of the aircraft around 200C (400F). Consequently, the fuel, the 80,000 lbs of fuel the SR-71 carried in its six main fuel tanks, would heat up to 190C (375F), just from the skin temperature due to friction with the air. This meant the chance of an explosion or a fire would be very high.

4

This meant that they had to develop a special fuel with a very high flashpoint, and this is where they came up with JP-7 which has a very high flashpoint.

A whole high-tech industry was created to provide the SR-71s sophisticated parts. The Soviet Union actually helped build the A-12 and SR-71. With both aircraft being made of 92% titanium inside and out. Back when they were building the aircraft the United States didn't have the ore supplies - an ore called rutile ore. It's a very sandy soil and is only found in very few parts of the world. The major supplier of the ore was the USSR. Working through Third World countries and bogus operations, they were able to get the rutile ore shipped to the United States to build the A-12 and SR-71.

As well as aircraft technology, it must not be forgotten that the main function of a spy plane is to take pictures. For this to be undertaken suitable cameras needed to be designed that could take clear pictures high up at very low temperatures. This in itself presented obstacles in terms of design that had to be overcome long before digital photography had been invented and pictures were taken on reels of film.

The Cold War helped rapid progress in both aviation and space technology. The drive to beat the Soviet Union in technology advances was a powerful motivator for America and its presidents. Without the Cold War it is highly likely that the U-2, A-12 and SR-71 would not have existed. The intelligence that both sides managed to gain was not always correct and always seemed to have claims that were slightly above the actuality. The Cold War began at the end of World War II starting, although the actual start is disputed amongst historians. British Prime Minister Winston Churchill was concerned that, given the enormous size of Soviet forces deployed in Europe at the end of the war, and the perception that Soviet leader Joseph Stalin was unreliable, there existed a Soviet threat to Western Europe. This book tells the development story of the U-2 and the SR-71 using recently declassified information on the projects and the use of Area 51 to keep the projects top secret. The best place to start is with a little background to the

Cold War, which would be the driving force behind the U-2 and later SR-71.

The Cold War, was initially driven by the Soviet Union wanting greater control of the countries that surrounded it to prevent invasion. From some viewpoints, it could be viewed that it is not too dissimilar to what is currently happening in Crimea and the Ukraine. However, under Stalin there was also the underlying issue of communism v capitalism. President Truman's advisers were concerned about the level of influence and control Starling was gaining in the Eastern Bloc, which were communist states of Central and Eastern Europe. The Soviet Union under the Warsaw pact (Treaty of Friendship, Co-operation, and Mutual Assistance) in 1955 had a defence strategy in place that concerned America and other western countries further. With all the concerns; this drove the need for intelligence so that either side to gain the upper hand. Spy networks were set up and Americas growing concern of the Soviet Union's nuclear capabilities drove the need for intelligence. This led to vast sums of money being poured into intelligence gathering- at a time before satellites the best way was to overfly and take pictures. With the increasing use of radar, anti-aircraft guns and missiles became harder and harder to achieve without more specialised aircraft that could either fly higher or faster to either avoid detection or avoid pursing missiles.

This book looks at that race to build an aircraft that could undertake dangerous overflight missions and keep both the aircraft and pilots that flew them, out of harm's way. This lead to the technologically ground breaking aircraft from the legendary Kelly Johnson and 'Lockheed Skunk Works.' Which would shape the future of aircraft design and at the same time pushed the need for more advanced radar and SAM missiles that could intercept at a much higher altitude on the Soviet side. The late 1950s and 60s saw technological advances not seen since World War II and many would say have not been seen since. The U-2 and later A-12 and SR-71would push technological boundaries and pave the way or more advanced if not quite as fast aircraft such as the

F-117A, B-2 and F-22 using data and lessons learnt from the U-2 and SR-71.

EDGE OF SPACE

If you were to look across Groom Lake in Nevada it looks almost inhospitable. With temperatures ranging from 52 degrees in the summer to -47 degrees in the winter it could be a harsh environment to live and work in. Overlooked by Bald Mountain, Groom Lake itself is nothing more than a dried up salt lake without a drop of water in sight. The nearest main roads, route 95 and route 375 run about 20 miles either side of Groom Lake. Groom Lake is of course next to Area 51 where several secret aircraft such as the A-12, SR-71 and F-117A amongst others have been tested. Area 51 is still a highly secret area, originally set up to develop highly secret aircraft starting with the U-2. The mystery and conspiracy theories surrounding Area 51, have been gathering momentum as the years have passed. Many have said that other than various secret conventional aircraft, and various captured foreign aircraft brought to Area 51 for testing. There has also been the constant rumours of alien craft and alien life forms, which in many ways have yet to be disproved or proved for that matter. It could be nothing more than a convenient cover to hide the testing of secret aircraft and associated systems.

These reports of aliens and alien raft have been rife since Area 51s inception; many have been proven to be nothing more than good cover stories to hide secret projects. Of course, there are the conspiracy theories and various cover up stories or even those wanting fame and fortune, which have muddied the truth further. This book is not about any of the alleged projects only the ones that have recently been declassified, which includes elements of the highly secretive Area 51.

***

It was mid-1956, when one of the first U-2 pilots pulled up to the gates of a heavily guarded Area 51. They had no idea of what aircraft they would be flying or even what the aircraft looked like. They were here, because curiosity had the better of them. When asked about flying some missions for the CIA - they were told they would have to become a civilian to do this. It was Eisenhower who wanted non-military pilots or 'drivers' as they would be known. Initially, foreign pilots were considered but due to the language barrier and other issues. These were deemed unsuitable and the preference was to recruit American pilots instead.

At the time, Area 51 had a small team from the now famous Lockheed Skunk Works, led by the legendary Kelly Johnson, with one of the sharpest minds in American aviation. His "down-to-brass-tacks" management style was summed up by his motto, "Be quick, be quiet, and be on time." With the P38 Lighting, P80 Shooting Star and F104 Starfighter under his belt, he had come up with an aeroplane that the USAF and CIA needed, even though initially the design had been rejected. His charisma and management style kept everyone on their toes and if he said something would be done by a set date, it would be. He had fourteen management rules that his workforce and even the test pilots were ruled by.

The Skunk Works manager must be delegated practically complete control of his program in all aspects. He should report to a division president or higher.

Strong but small project offices must be provided both by the military and industry.

The number of people having any connection with the project must be restricted in an almost vicious manner. Use a small number of good people (10% to 25% compared to the so-called normal systems).

A very simple drawing and drawing release system with great flexibility for making changes must be provided.

There must be a minimum number of reports required, but important work must be recorded thoroughly.

There must be a monthly cost review covering not only what has been spent and committed but also projected costs to the conclusion of the program. Don't have the books 90 days late, and don't surprise the customer with sudden overruns.

The contractor must be delegated and must assume more than normal responsibility to get good vendor bids for subcontract on the project. Commercial bid procedures are very often better than military ones.

The inspection system as currently used by the Skunk Works, which has been approved by both the Air Force and Navy, meets the intent of existing military requirements and should be used on new projects. Push more basic inspection responsibility back to subcontractors and vendors. Don't duplicate so much inspection.

The contractor must be delegated the authority to test his final product in flight. He can and must test it in the initial stages. If he doesn't, he rapidly loses his competency to design other vehicles.

The specifications applying to the hardware must be agreed to well in advance of contracting. The Skunk Works practice of having a specification section stating clearly which important military specification items will not knowingly be complied with and reasons therefore is highly recommended.

Funding a program must be timely so that the contractor doesn't have to keep running to the bank to support government projects.

There must be mutual trust between the military project organization and the contractor with very close cooperation and liaison on a day-to-day basis. This cuts down misunderstanding and correspondence to an absolute minimum.
Access by outsiders to the project and its personnel must be strictly controlled by appropriate security measures.

Because only a few people will be used in engineering and most other areas, ways must be provided to reward good performance by pay not based on the number of personnel supervised.

Kelly had a 15th rule that he passed on by word of mouth. "Starve before doing business with the damned Navy. They don't know what the hell they want and will drive you up a wall before they break either your heart or a more exposed part of your anatomy."

Kelly Johnson

To see Kelly Johnson at work was simply amazing. He would have a solution to a problem that had not occurred. He was a perfectionist when it came to his aircraft. He was not always right and even though he did not really like it; he was happy to be proved wrong. Some of his ideas were so simple yet so effective such as his approach to prototype development. Where he would have his engineers and draftsmen located not more than 50 feet from the aircraft assembly line. This meant that any difficulties in construction were immediately brought to the attention of the engineers, who were then able gather the mechanics around the drafting tables and discuss ways to overcome any difficulties. Thus, engineers were generally able to fix problems in the design in a matter of hours, not days or weeks. There was also no emphasis placed on producing neatly typed memorandums; engineers simply made pencil notations on the drawings to ensure solutions could be undertaken as quickly as possible.

Clarence Leonard "Kelly" Johnson was born on 27 February 1910. His nickname "Kelly" came from when he was at grade school in

Michigan. He was constantly ridiculed for his name, Clarence. Some of the boys started calling him "Clara". Then one morning while waiting in line to get into a classroom, one boy started with the normal routine of calling him "Clara". Johnson decided to trip him up, and it was so hard that the boy he tripped up broke his leg. The rest of the boys at school, then decided that he wasn't a "Clara" after all, and started calling him "Kelly". The nickname came from the popular song at the time, "Kelly with the Green Neck Tie." From that point forward, he was always known as "Kelly" Johnson.

Whilst at the University of Michigan, Kelly Johnson conducted a series of wind tunnel tests of Lockheed's proposed twin-engine Lockheed Model 10 Electra airliner. Kelly found that the aircraft did not have adequate directional stability, but his professor felt it did and reported so to Lockheed. Upon completing his master's degree in 1933, Johnson joined the Lockheed Company as a tool designer at a salary of $83 a month. Shortly after starting at Lockheed, Johnson convinced Hall Hibbard, the chief engineer, that the Lockheed Model 10 Electra was unstable. Hibbard sent Johnson back to Michigan to conduct more tests. Johnson eventually made multiple changes to the wind tunnel model, including adding an "H" tail, to address the problem. Lockheed accepted Kelly's suggestions and the Model 10 went on to be a success. This brought Kelly to the attention of Lockheed management, and he was promoted to aeronautical engineer. He stayed with Lockheed forming the now famous Skunk Works until his retirement from Lockheed as a senior vice president in 1975, although he continued as a consultant to the Skunk Works after his retirement.

U-2 Development

The story of the U-2 and Area 51 began on May 1, 1954, when leaders across Washington D.C.'s intelligence community found themselves breaking out in a cold, panicked sweat. Over the skies of Red Square in Moscow, the Soviet Union had just introduced its newest bomber — the Myasishchev M-4, ominously nicknamed "Hammer" — during a Russian May Day celebration. Coming on the heels of the Soviet Union's successful detonation of a hydrogen bomb the previous summer. The unveiling fuelled a growing fear that Russia had not only eclipsed the West in terms of both nuclear weapons and bomber production, but was gearing up for a potential attack on America as well. American grew more fearful of Russia and desperately needed intelligence to find out exactly what capabilities' the Soviets had. The Cold War had begun overnight at the end of World War Two and the Soviet Union had changed from a strong ally to become America's fiercest Cold War rival. The only way to find out what the Russians were up to was to penetrate the iron curtain.

Which was easier said than done, simply due to the vast size of the Soviet Union and the ground to air capabilities the Soviet's had. Any allied aircraft that had gone too close to Russian airspace had been quickly shot down. There was a clear and present danger that needed to be addressed and the only way for this to happen was by gathering intelligence. To gather intelligence a high-altitude aircraft was needed. One that could fly vast distances, high above Soviet fighters and ground to air missiles whilst taking photographs.

The highest-flying aircraft available in America at the time was the English Electric Canberra, which had a service ceiling of 48,000 feet. The USAF asked English Electric's help to help further modify the American licensed version of the Canberra, known as the Martin B-57. The plan was to add long, thin wings, new engines, and a lighter-than-normal airframe to reach 67,000 feet. Although in the end the RB-57D was only able to reach 64,000 feet after Air Research and Development Command mandated changes to the design, which although made the aircraft more durable during wartime. It also reduces the height the

RB-57D could fly at, meaning in the end it could only reach 64,000 feet.

The thought was that if an aircraft could fly at 70,000 feet it would be beyond the reach of Soviet fighters, missiles, and radar. John Seaberg a US Air Force officer, wrote in 1953 a request for proposal for an aircraft that could reach 70,000 feet over a target with 1,500 nautical miles of operational radius. With many aviation companies already involved in the design and production of other aircraft the USAF decided the contract would only be awarded to smaller companies who would give the project greater attention. The project was given the name "Bald Eagle" and contracts were given to Bell Aircraft, Martin Aircraft and Fairchild to develop proposals for a new reconnaissance aircraft. Lockheed got wind of the project and decided to submit a proposal even though they had not been approached. Kelly Johnson was asked to come up with a design.

One thought by a Lockheed executive John H Carter was to not have any undercarriage to further save weight, which would increase the altitude the aircraft could fly at. Kelly Johnson's design proposal, called the CL-282. It would take the body from the F104 Starfighter currently in development along with a General Electric J37 engine and long glider like wings. It was a jet powered glider and would take off from a dolly and land on skids. It could reach 70,000 feet with a 2,000-mile range.

The USAF rejected the design and instead went with the Bell X-16 and modified B-57. The reason given was due to the lack of landing gear, engine choice and only being a single engine design. The X-16 was later cancelled in favour of the B-57 that eventually could only fly at a maximum height of 64,000 feet and led to the Lockheed CL-282 design being reconsidered. The CL-282 already had some fans who were impressed by its low radar cross section and the height it could fly at. Trevor Gardner, an aide to Secretary of the Air Force Harold E. Talbott, recommended the design to the CIA's Office of Scientific Intelligence. Allen Donovan, a sailplane enthusiast who believed that a sailplane was the type of high-altitude aircraft the Office of Scientific

Intelligence were seeking. The CL-282 would however be fitted with the more powerful Pratt & Whitney J57 engine. Lockheed had, however become busy with other projects and had to be persuaded to take on the contract after it had been approved. The CL-282 was renamed U-2 to help hide what it was. The U stood for Utility and there was already a U-1 and U-3, so seemed a good way to further hide a secret plane from Russia.

Richard M Bissell was pointed head of the project. Covert funding was used and Lockheed received a $22.5 Million contract for the first 20 aircraft. Lockheed via Kelly Johnson agreed to deliver the first aircraft by July 1956 and the last by November 1956. It helped that the aircraft was based on the F-104 with only the wings and tail being different. This speeded up the process and brought the contract in under budget by $3.5 million. There were technical challenges ahead, such as stopping the fuel from boiling at such a high altitude. Petroleum company, Shell had to develop a special fuel for high altitude flight. To conduct lengthy missions over hostile territory, the U-2 needed to carry a large amount of fuel. Kelly Johnson used a "wet-wing" design for the U-2, which meant that fuel was not stored in separate fuel tanks but rather in the wing itself. Each wing was then divided into two leak proof compartments, and fuel was pumped into all the cavities within these areas; only the outer 6 feet of the wings were not used for fuel storage. The U-2 also had a 100-gallon reserve tank in its nose. Later, in 1957, Kelly Johnson increased the fuel capacity of the U-2 by adding 100-gallon "slipper" tanks under each wing, projecting slightly ahead of the leading edge.

One of the most important considerations in the U-2's fuel system was for the need to maintain aircraft trim as the fuel was consumed. Balancing of the U-2 was crucial to keep it stable during high altitude flight. The aircraft therefore contained a complex system of feed lines and valves draining to a central sump, which made it impossible to provide the pilot with an empty/full type of fuel gauge. None of the first 50 U-2s had normal fuel gauges. Instead, there were mechanical fuel totalizer/counters. Before the start of a mission, the ground crew set the counters to indicate the total amount of fuel in the wings, and then a flow meter subtracted the gallons of fuel actually consumed during the flight the pilot kept a log of the fuel consumption shown by the counters and compared it with estimates made by mission planners for each leg of the flight As a double check, U-2 pilots also kept track of their fuel consumption by monitoring airspeed and time in the air.

In designing the U-2 aircraft, Kelly Johnson was confronted with two major problems-fuel capacity and weight. To achieve an intercontinental range, the aircraft had to carry a large supply of fuel, yet it also had to be light enough to attain the ultra-high altitudes needed to be safe from interception. Although the final product resembled a typical jet aircraft, its construction was unlike any other US military aircraft. One unusual design feature was the tail assembly, which-to save weight-was attached to the main body with just three tension bolts. This feature had been adapted from sailplane designs.

The wings were also unique. Unlike conventional aircraft, whose main wing spar passes through the fuselage to give the wings continuity and strength, the U-2 had two separate wing panels. Which were attached to the fuselage sides with tension bolts (again, just as in sail- planes). Because the wing spar did not pass through the fuselage, Johnson was able to locate the camera behind the pilot and ahead of the engine, thereby improving the aircraft's centre of gravity and reducing its weight.

The wings were the most challenging design features of the entire aircraft. Their combination of high-aspect ratio and low-drag ratio, meant they were very long, narrow and thin just like a glider. Which made them unique in jet aircraft design. The wings were essentially integral fuel tanks that carried almost all of the U-2's fuel supply.

The wings and tail section were quite fragile. This fragility forced Kelly Johnson to look for a way to project the aircraft from gusts of wind at altitudes below 35,000 feet, which otherwise might cause the aircraft to disintegrate. Johnson looked at sailplane designs to devise what he called "gust control." This mechanism sets the ailerons and horizontal stabilizers into a position that kept the aircraft in a slightly nose-up attitude, so that any sudden stresses caused by the wind were greatly reduced. The U-2 still required expert handling on the part of the pilot though. Another design feature was the lightweight bicycle type landing gear. It was made from a single oleostrut and fitted with two lightweight wheels towards the front of the aircraft and two solid mounted wheels under the tail section. Together they only weighed 208 pounds, but were still able to withstand the landing from the seven-ton U-2. With both wheels located underneath the fuselage, two extra stabilizers were required at the end of the very long wings to keep them level during take-off. These 'pogos' as they were called were long curved metal sticks with a wheel on them. The pogos were detached from the aircraft by the pilot immediately after take-off. The wing also had skids on its tips to aid in landing of the U-2.

The other issues included stopping the pilot's blood from boiling at high altitude. Above 65,000 feet the body's fluids vaporize. Furthermore, the reduced atmospheric pressure placed considerable stress on the pilot's cardiovascular system and would not provide adequate oxygenation of the blood. This meant a totally different approach would be needed to keep the pilot alive at the high altitudes for a long period of time during the overflights. A system needed to be developed that could maintain pressure over much of the pilot's body. Once developed the technology would go on to play a major role in the manned space program. A Dr. Lovelace had begun his research on high-altitude flight before World War Two and was a co-inventor of the standard Air Force oxygen mask. In the early 1950s, he and Colonel Donald Flickinger made daring parachute jumps from B-47 bombers to test pilot-survival gear under extreme conditions Flickinger and Lovelace suggested that the Agency asks the David Clark Company of Worcester, Massachusetts, a manufacturer of environmental suits for Air Force pilots to submit designs for more advanced equipment for the pilots of the new aircraft. David Clark expert, Joseph Ruseckas then developed for the time, a complex life-support system, which was the first partially pressurized space suit. Along with the pressurized suits the Firewall Company of Buffalo,

New York pressurized the cockpit so that at high altitude it was the equivalent of 28,000 feet.

The components required to build the U2 were procured in secret. One example is for the U2's altimeters that needed to be calibrated to 80,000 feet and their current highest model was calibrated to 45,000 feet. The CIA set up a cover story about experimental rocket aircraft. The CIA assigned the cryptonym "Aquatone" to the project, with the USAF using the name "Oilstone" for their support to the CIA during the project. The cameras that were to be carried by the U2 were designed by James Baker whilst working for Perkin-Elmer. The cameras had a resolution of 2.5 feet from an altitude of 60,000 feet. The lens used in the U2s cameras was a 180-inch f/13.85 lens in a 13" by 13" format. The final part of the design to ensure the U-2 stayed balanced when the cameras were rolling, was to have one reel one side feeding forward while those on the other side feeding backward, thus maintaining a balanced weight distribution whilst the cameras were rolling. The lightweight construction and large wings meant that the U-2 airframe could easily be ripped apart if not kept within its flight envelope. At high altitude, the U-2 was so streamlined it could easily pick up speed and had to be flown with the nose slightly upwards to keep a steady speed. Airspeed was a very critical factor for the U-2. At maximum altitude, only 6 knots separated the speeds at which low-speed stall and high-speed buffet occurred. Pilot's called this narrow range of acceptable airspeeds at maximum altitude the "coffin corner" because at this point the U-2 was always on the brink of falling out of the sky. If the aircraft slowed beyond the low-speed stall limit it would lose lift and begin to fall. Causing stresses that would tear the wings and tail off. A little too much speed would lead to buffeting. Which would also cause the loss of the wings or tail.

AREA 51

On 12 April 1955, Richard Bissell and Colonel Osmund Ritland who was the senior Air Force officer for the project staff. Flew over Nevada looking for suitable testing facilities with Kelly Johnson in a small Beechcraft plane, piloted by Lockheed's chief test pilot, Tony LeVier. They spotted what appeared to be an airstrip by a salt flat known as Groom Lake, near the northeast corner of the Atomic Energy Commission's Nevada Proving Ground. After debating about landing on the old airstrip, LeVier set the plane down on the lakebed, and all four walked over to examine the strip. The facility was used during World War II as an aerial gunnery range for Army Air Corps pilots. On the face of it looked an ideal site and from the air the strip appeared to be paved. However, on closer inspection the paved runway was fashioned from compacted earth that over the past decade of disuse had turned into almost ankle deep dust.

After discussion, they concluded it would be an ideal facility for both the testing and training of its pilots. It was an isolated location away from prying eyes and fear of Soviet spies. Groom Lake turned out to not be owned by the Atomic Energy Commission, so Bissell and Miller asked for it to be added to the Atomic Energy's real estate to which they agreed. President Eisenhower also agreed to a strip of wasteland known as 'Area 51' due to its map co-ordinates being added to enlarge the facility. To make the new facility in the middle of nowhere sound more attractive to his workers, Kelly Johnson called it the Paradise Ranch, which was soon shortened to the 'Ranch'. It was decided to build a proper runway rather than re-compacting the ground to create a runway. The base was ready by July 1955 and was just a series of hangers and workshop facilities for housing the U-2. On 25 July, Kelly Johnson was ready to deliver the first aircraft known as article 341, to Area 51. With its long, slender wings and tail assembly removed. The aircraft was wrapped in tarpaulins, loaded aboard a C-124, and flown to Groom Lake. Where Lockheed mechanics spent the next six days readying the craft for its first flight.

The taxing trials began on 27 July 1957 when LeVier took the U-2 up to 50 knots on the runway. A second taxing trial followed on 1 August, were LeVier accelerated the U-2 to 70 knots and began to try the ailerons. It was at this point that he became aware of being airborne. LeVier was amazed at how easily the U-2 had taken unintentionally to the air. He immediately tried to get the U-2 back on the ground, but had difficulty determining his height because the lakebed had no markings to judge distance or height. When he finally made contact with the ground in a left bank of approximately 10 degrees." The U-2 bounced back into the air, but LeVier was able to bring it back down for a second landing. He then applied the brakes with little effect, and the aircraft rolled for a long distance before finally coming to a stop. Kelly Johnson saw the aircraft fall and bounce along with Bissell and Cunningham. All three leapt into a Jeep and headed off towards the U-2. They caught up with the U-2 with its brakes on fire. They quickly extinguished the fire, shouting at LeVier to get out. LeVier later complained about the poor brakes and lack of markings on the runway. The unintentional flight would prove how easy the U-2 could take off, but also how difficult it was to land due to the ground effect of its highly efficient glider like wings.

Tony LeVier was born Anthony Puck in Duluth, Minnesota, on 14 February 1913. His father died while he was still young. His mother remarried when he was a teenager, to Oscar LeVier, who then gave the children his surname. LeVier from an early had been much more interested in flying than his studies, so he dropped out of high school to pursue flying full time. To pay for food and flying, he worked several jobs maintaining aircraft or undertaking flight instruction. In 1936, Levier turned his hand to Airacing, then after the war he brought a surplus P-38 Lightning, which he modified and painted red. Winning the national air races in Cleveland and coming second in the Thompson Trophy. In between his air racing, Le Vier worked as an airline pilot and mechanic before ending up Ferrying Hudson bombers and the Lodestar transport variant for Lockheed, to the RAF in England.

In 1942 his title changed to engineering test pilot when he began to fly the PV-1 Ventura. LeVier played an important part proving the P-38 Lightning design. Undertaking numerous flights testing its dive and speed ability. After the P-39, LeVier went on to test the P-80 shooting star, America's first operational jet fighter. He tested two variants of the P-80. The T-33 and the three variants of the F-94 Starfire. He also performed most of the tests of the XF-90 penetration fighter prototype and flew the first flights of the XF-104 Starfighter, and the U-2.

Taxi trials on the U-2, continued in earnest once the damaged tires, brake and oleostrut on the undercarriage had been repaired. The first planned flight was on 4 August 1955. LeVier would again fly the U-2, he had been instructed by Kelly Johnson to land the U-2 by making initial contact with the main or forward landing gear and then let the plane settle back on the rear wheel. LeVier disagreed with this approach; he said that the U-2 would bounce if he tried to land like this. After taking the U-2 up to 8,000 feet and cycling through the undercarriage going up and down several times along with the flaps, LeVier returned to Groom Lake to attempt a landing. He tried unsuccessfully four times, to land the U-2 front wheel first and each time it would bounce back in the air. He then finally decided to try it his way and land rear wheels first, making a near perfect landing. Which was only 10 minutes before a sudden thunderstorm dumped about 2 inches of rain and flooded both Groom Lake and the runway.

The official first flight with guests of the U-2 was to be 8 August 1955. This time the U-2 flew to 32,000 feet and flew with no issues. This in turn meant Kelly Johnson had met the tight 8-month deadline to get the first aircraft into the air. LeVier made another 19 flights in the U-2 before he was moved onto other Lockheed projects. Successive flights tested the maximum speed of Mack 0.85 along with taking the U-2 up to greater heights, before reaching its design altitude of 65,000 feet on the 8 September 1955.

It was on the on 22 September 1955 the U-2 experienced its first flameout at 64,000 feet or more than 12 miles high. After a brief restart, the J57/P-37 engine again flamed out at 60,000 feet, and the U-

2 descended to 35,000 feet before the engine could be relit. Pratt & Whitney engineers immediately set out to find a solution to the problem. The P-37 model engine had significantly poorer combustion characteristics than the preferred but currently unavailable P-31 version - therefore tended to flame out at high altitudes. Combustion problems usually became apparent as the U-2 began the final part of its climb at about 57,000 to 65,000 feet, causing pilots to refer to this area as the "bad- lands" or the "chimney." Flameouts continued to cause issues for the U-2 until sufficient numbers of the more powerful P-31 engines became available in the spring of 1956. One such Flameout occurred during final tests in the spring of 1956, where the U-2 once again demonstrated its unique airworthiness. On 14 April 1956, James Cunningham was sitting in his office in Washington when he received a call from Area 51, informing him that a westward-bound U-2 had experienced a flameout over the Mississippi River at the western border of Tennessee. After restarting his engine, the pilot reported having a second flameout and engine vibrations so violent that he was unable to get the engine to start again. Bissell and Ritland had foreseen such an emergency early in the project, and with the cooperation of the Air Force, had arranged for sealed orders to be delivered to every airbase in continental United States, giving instructions about what to do if a U-2 needed to make an emergency landing.

Cunningham had the project office asked the pilot how far he could glide so they could determine which Strategic Air Command (SAC) base should be alerted. The pilot by this time was over Arkansas; radioed back that given the prevailing winds and the U-2's glide ability, he thought he could reach Albuquerque, New Mexico. Within minutes, Cunningham was on the phone to a Colonel Geary in the Pentagon, who then had the Air Force's Assistant Director of Operations on the phone. Brigadier General Koon, called the commander of Kirtland AFB near Albuquerque. General Koon told the base commander about the sealed orders and explained that an unusual aircraft would make a dead stick landing at Kirtland within the next half hour. The general then instructed the base commander to have air police keep everyone away from the craft and get it inside a hanger as quickly as possible.

After a half hour passed, the base commander called the Pentagon to ask where the crippled aircraft was. As he was speaking, the officer saw the U-2 touch down on the runway and remarked, "It's not a plane, it's a glider!" Even more surprised were the air police who surrounded the craft when it came to a halt. As the pilot climbed from the cockpit in his "space suit," one air policeman remarked that the pilot looked like a man from Mars. The pilot later reported to Cunningham that from the beginning of the first flameout until the landing at Albuquerque, the U-2 had covered over 900 miles. Including more than 300 miles gliding.

Aside from this extraordinary gliding ability, the U-2 was a very difficult aircraft to fly. Being lightweight, enabled it to achieve extreme altitude, also made it very fragile. The aircraft was also very sleek, and it sliced through the air with very little drag. This feature was dangerous, however, because the U-2 was not built to withstand the G-forces of high speed. Pilots had to be extremely careful to keep the craft in a slightly nose-up attitude when flying at operational altitude. If the nose dropped only a degree or two in a nose down position, the plane would gain speed at a dramatic rate, exceeding the placarded speed limit in less than a minute, at which point the aircraft would begin to come apart. Pilots therefore had to pay close attention to the aircraft's speed indicator because at 65,000 feet there was no physical sensation of speed, without objects close at hand for the eye to use as a reference.

Meanwhile, with the airworthiness of the U-2 airframe proven, Lockheed set up a production line in the Skunk Works, but delivery of even the second-choice 157/P-37 engines became a major problem. Pratt & Whitney's was already at full production of these engines for the next year. They were contracted to the Air Force to produce engines, for use in F-1 00 and KC-135 tankers. The only way around this was to divert a small number of engines to the U-2 project with the help of Colonel Geary and a colleague to enable production of the U-2 to continue. As more U-2s arrived at Area 51, more Lockheed staff was needed there and it was thought that the best way round this was to fly the workers in on a Monday and then return them to on a Friday. A Military Air Transport Service (MATS) using a USAF C-54 aircraft began on 3 October 1955 bringing essential personnel in and out of Area. Sadly, less than seven weeks after it started, a MATS aircraft bound for Area 51 crashed on 17 November. Killing all 14 persons aboard the plane, including the Project Security Officer. The CIA's William H Marr along with four members of his staff, and personnel from Lockheed and Hycon also died in the crash.

This crash would represent the greatest single loss of life in the entire U-2 program. Testing of the U-2 continued and as more flights took place, the first reports of UFO's started to come in. At the time, most passenger aircraft flew at around 10,000-20,000 feet and military aircraft like the B-57 at around 40,000 feet. Therefore, to see something flying so high it could only be a UFO. Such reports were most prevalent in the early evening from pilots of airliners flying from east to west. When the sun dropped below the horizon of an airliner flying at 20,000 feet the plane was in darkness. But, if a U-2 was airborne near the airliner at the same its horizon from an altitude of 60.000 feet its bare metal body would catch the sun causing it to glint and appear as it was almost on fire to the airline some 40,000 feet below. Even during the day, the U2s silver fuselage and wings would catch the sun and send strange flashes of light as the sun caught them and sunlight bounced off the U-2s shiny fuselage. Not only did the airline pilots report their sightings to air-traffic controllers. They, along with ground-based observers wrote letters to the Air Force unit at Wright Air Development Command in Dayton charged with investigating such phenomena. This, in turn, led to the Air Force's Operation BLUE BOOK. Based at Wright-Patterson airfield, the operation collected all reports of UFO sightings. Air Force investigators then attempted to explain such sightings by linking them to natural phenomena. BLUE BOOK investigators regularly called on the Agency's Project Staff in Washington to check reported UFO sightings against U-2 flight logs. This enabled the investigators to eliminate most the UFO reports, although they could not reveal to the letter writers the true cause of the UFO sightings. U-2 and later OXCART (Lockheed A-12) flights accounted for more than one-half of all UFO reports during the late 1950s and most of the 1960s. With Roswell, still, very fresh in people's minds, the conspiracy theories grew and grew and some even had an element of truth. With suggestions, Alien craft were taking off and landing at Area 51. Although the Alien element was simply highly secret aircraft. In many ways, the UFO/Alien sightings and theories were excellent cover stories about what was really being undertaken at Area 51.

PILOT TRAINING

Below is an account from an unnamed U-2 pilot, undergoing their flight training and first flight in the U2.

"It was May 1956 that I began my training on the U-2. When I got my first glimpse of the U-2 in its hanger. It looked very much like an F-104 that had had glider wings stuck on it. The wings looked as though they would fall off the minute it got airborne. It did have its own beauty from the rounded nose to the long, slender wings that reminded me of a soaring eagle.

Even before the recruiting effort had gotten under way the Air Force and CIA had begun to develop a pilot training program for the U-2. Under the terms of the OILSTONE agreement between the Agency and the Air Force, responsibility for pilot training lay squarely with SAC. This essential activity was carried out under the supervision of Col William F Yancey who was assigned to March AFB and flew to nearby Area 51 each day. Colonel Yancey oversaw six SAC pilots who were to be trained by Lockheed test pilots to fly the U-2. Once they became qualified, these SAC pilots would become the trainers for us "sheep-dipped" former Reserve SAC pilots. Who would then go on to fly U-2 missions for the CIA.

The Air Force transition team developed a complete program of ground school and flying, which started with several low-level flights with pogos attached on the U-2. During this time, all of them went to David Clark in the northeast to have our partial pressure suits fitted for high altitude flight. The program progressed quite rapidly with the LAC and Air Force team learning more about the U-2 through daily flights. With us student pilots following closely behind, gaining proficiency with each ground school class and training flights. The U-2 took some mastering and whilst easy to fly, was not forgiving if you did not take care and fly within its flight envelope.

Upon completion of the training program, each of us was declared mission and combat capable. There were no course failures, since we were all very skilled pilots and would not have been selected for the program had we not been. The initial selection had been vigorous and they wanted pilots who had extensive flying experience.

LeVier as the first test pilot of the U-2, trained several other Lockheed test pilots in the difficult art of flying the U-2. Eventually there were enough trained Lockheed pilots available to test the aircraft coming off the assembly line and at the same time train the SAC pilots. Training was difficult because there was no two-seat model of the U-2. All instruction we had, had to be given on the ground before takeoff and then over the radio once the craft was airborne. On paper, it was a very simple aircraft to fly, however, became a very complex aircraft to fly once at high altitudes or landing. The U-2 required a pilot's full attention when not using the autopilot. Airspeed was such a critical factor that Kelly Johnson added a vernier adjustment to the throttle to allow us to make minute alterations to the fuel supply. The U-2 was a mixture of a glider and a jet and could not survive the stresses of loops and barrel rolls. The original U-2s were placarded, which meant that they could not be flown at sea level faster than 190 knots in smooth air or 150 knots in rough air. At operational altitude where the air was much less dense, they could not exceed Mach 0.8. Speeds in excess of these limits could cause the wings or tail section to fall off.

Among the unique devices developed for the U-2 was a small sextant for making celestial "fixes" during the long overflights. Because cloud cover often prevented U-2 pilots from locating navigational points on the earth through the periscope. The sextant turned out to be our principal navigational instrument during the first three years of deployment. When the clouds were not a factor, the periscope proved highly accurate for navigation. During the final tests before the aircraft became operational, we found we could navigate by dead reckoning with an error of less than one nautical mile over a 1000 nautical mile course.

The worst part about flying the U-2 though was the early pressure suits. The MC-2 and MC-3 partial-pressure suits were very uncomfortable to wear especially over long periods of time. To prevent loss of pressure, we had to wear a heavy coverall, that had to fit tightly at the wrists and ankles as the hands and feet were initially not pressurised. We also had to wear gloves and a heavy helmet that tended to chafe your neck and shoulders. It was also prone to fogging. Problems with the life-support system were believed to have been the cause of several of early crashes of the U-2, as pilots blacked out at high altitude.

Once we had the bulky suit on and had been shoehorned into the cockpit, the next problem was how to get out in an emergency. The U-2 cockpit was very small, and the early models did not even have an ejection seat. To save weight, the first seats fitted to the U-2 were extremely simple with no height adjustment mechanism. They had been designed for pilots of above-average height. The only way to adjust the seat for slightly shorter pilots like myself was to insert wooden blocks beneath the seat to adjust it. For later versions of the aircraft, Kelly Johnson added a fully adjustable seat.

The Air Force undertook bailout experiments at high altitudes from balloons in the autumn of 1955 to determine if the suit designed for flying the U-2 would also protect us during our parachute descent, once we were separated from the life-support mechanisms inside the U-2. Even though the descent would be quick hypoxia due to lack of oxygen, would be the greatest threat along with the 'bends' and the suit had to keep us alive. The parachute would deploy automatically at a set height if we did become unconscious. At higher altitudes, we were to fly at, the "bends" was a real issue. The "bends" also known as Decompression sickness is when dissolved gases come out of solution into bubbles inside the body on depressurisation. Its effects may vary from joint pain and rashes to paralysis and death. To avoid this, we had to put on our pressure suits and begin breathing pure oxygen 90 minutes before our flight. Two reasons for the bends are Boyle's law and Armstrong's line. Boyle's law is that a given quantity of gas varies proportionately with the amount of pressure exerted upon it. At the lower altitudes that humans normally live, we are used to 14.7 pounds of pressure per square inch (psi) at sea level. Sea level can be thought of as the bottom of the air as opposed to the sea. Air itself does have its own weight. This weight decreases with altitude as the air gets thinner. The pound's psi at altitude is less than a half-pound. Armstrong's line says that at 63,000 feet pressure altitude, conventional liquids boil at 98 degrees Fahrenheit. If the pilot were exposed to the environment at 70,000 feet, the gases in their body would rapidly expand or boil causing it to explode - causing instant death.

I was lucky never to experience the bends, but those that did said it could quite painful. One pilot told me that the bubbles went to his frontal lobe and it almost blinded him; before he blacked out for a short period. After which he managed to safely land, but never flew the U-2 again. Once in these pressure suits eating and drinking was a major problem as was urinating. The earlier suits had no provision for urination making long flights quite uncomfortable. Once our pre-breathing had been completed, we would then be taken out to our U-2 in an air-conditioned truck, which was very much needed in the heat of Groom Lake, which could reach 100 degrees. The U-2s had external sun visors fitted to them which were removed just prior to take off to give us some respite from the sun. It was still a very hot place to be on the ground for too long - it was always nice to get airborne and up into cooler air."

FIRST FLIGHT

A typical high altitude flight is involved. The day prior a flight, two drivers were identified, as a primary and a backup. The backup pilot is also called a mobile officer. The mobile officer has two roles. The first is as a safety observer/mission monitor and secondly, he will become the mission pilot if the primary driver becomes incapacitated for any reason. Every mission was thoroughly planned, even routine test flights.

On the day of the actual flight, the pilot and mobile officer show up a couple of hours prior to our take off time. We would then receive a weather brief and an intelligence brief, if it was an overflight mission. Finally, is a high protein meal of something like Steak and Eggs to ensure our bodies have the necessary energy to withstand a long flight.

Following the meal, the primary pilot receives a physical exam. During this exam, the doctor checks your pulse rate, blood pressure, body temperature, ears, and your nose and throat are scrutinized to ensure that you are fit and ready to endure the high-altitude flight environment for several hours. Finally, the pilot would climb on the back of an air-conditioned truck which will take you out to your awaiting U-2.

On arrival at the U-2, the pilot would get out of the back of the truck and walked towards the U-2 for my first flight. Once I had signed part 2 of the 781 form, ground staff helped to get the pilot into the cockpit and do up all the straps, before the pilot then made sure the capstan and bladder hoses were attached and the primary aircraft oxygen system was on. They would then continue with various checks to the radio and oxygen systems along with a radio check. By today's standards the cockpit was not that complex with a raft of analogue dials now replaced by multiple screens in later generations of aircraft. There was still a large number of dials and switches though, all needed to make and keep the U-2 flying. A lengthy pre-flight checklist need to be followed prior to take off.

Inverter - ON, LIGHT OUT

MA1 compass - SLAVED

Radio compass - ANTENA
Flight plan - FILED
Anti Collision switch - ON
Fan Checked and - OFF
Seal valves – ON
Landing lights checked and – OFF
Emergency fuel shutdown – COVER DOWN
Gust control – FAIRED
Wing flap switch – UP
Friction Lock – ADJUSTED
Throttle – OFF
Speed brake switch – FORWARD
Left Canopy jettison HANDLE – ALIGNED AND SAFETIED
Oxygen pressure – CHECKED
Fuel transfer switch – OFF
Gear handle – DOWN WARNING SYTEM CHECKED
Fuel transfer switch – OFF
Drag chute handle – IN
Ram air switch – OFF
Face heat – SET
Cabin heat selector – AUTO
Cabin temperature – SET
Generator battery switch – OFF
Pitot Heat – OFF
AC alternator switch – ON
Master watch – INSTALLED
Aircraft clock – SET
Emergency face plate heater circuit breaker – PULLED
All other circuit breakers – SET
Fuel totalizer – SET
Sump overflow light – ILLUMINATED
Instrument and panel lights – SET
Emergency fuel control switch – NORMAL
Destructor – SAFETIED

Push to test lights – CHECKED

Autopilot – CHECKED AND OFF

Equipment master switch – OFF

Equipment mode selector – OFF

Defroster – OFF

Cover jettison switch – COVER DOWN

Hatch heater switch – OFF

Altimeter selector switch – EQUIPMENT BAY

Trim power switch – ON

Trim tabs – CHECKED AND NEUTRAL

Rudder pedals – ADJUSTED

Cockpit auxiliary lights – SET

Flashlight – CHECKED

Mission special equipment – SET

Oxygen quick disconnect – CHECKED

Suit connections – CHECKED

Low altitude escape lanyard – HOOKED

Face plate latch – LOCKED

Emergency face heat cord – CONECTED

Green apple – SECURE

Ground staff disconnects headset and turns recorder switch – OFF

Radio bypass chord – STORED

Radio compass – CHECKED

Canopy – CLOSED AND LOCKED

Yaw string – FREE

Ladder - Removed

The next step was to start the single engine, which is done by an orthodox ground starting system powered via an air hose attached to the U-2. The air hose must be removed by the ground staff prior to take off. The air supply windmills the engine before you press and hold the starter button and wait for the engine to ignite, which you can see by a rise in the Exhaust Gas Temperature (EGT) gauge and a rise in oil pressure. If it does not rise within 30 seconds of depressing the button, you must wait while any excess fuel is dispersed and then try again.

Once the engine is running, it is a case of checking the RPM gauge before doing a final check of all the gauges, setting the flaps to zero, checking flight controls and switching the fan on. Ground staff, then check the anti-collision lights are on, engine access doors are closed, landing gear pins are removed before removing the wheel chocks and a final check to see the taxi route is clear.

Only a very slight push on the throttle will have the U-2 moving forward on its taxi run towards the runway at about 30 knots. Taxing the U-2 is challenging. Turning into the wind, the turn radius is about 189 feet. Turning away from the wind, the turn radius can exceed 300 feet. You need to judge turns carefully or you can easily find yourself getting stuck. Which means the aircraft needing to be repositioned by the ground crew. To put the U-2s turning circle into perspective a typical fighter plane of the day would have had a turning circle of around 20-50 feet. During this activity, the mobile officer follows along in a high-performance chase car. The mobile officer is in constant radio contact with the pilot, and he has the role of safety observer, monitoring the aircraft as it moves.

The pre-flight check is so extensive as there is very little time from starting takeoff to being airborne and performing quite a steep climb. Once lined up at the end of the runway and final clearance has been given. You push the throttle slowly forward to about 70% to avoid any 'chugging' from the engine then push to 85% throttle before releasing the brakes and pushing the throttle to 100%. The control stick needs to be pushed forward as you begin to accelerate down the runway and make use of the tail wheel steering until the tail lifts up. At about 50 knots, the wings begin to rise and the pogos will fall off. At 70 knots the tail begins to rise and the control column needs to be pulled back to keep the tail wheel about a foot from the runway. Only a slight pull back on the control column is needed for the U-2 to become airborne. Actual takeoff speed varies between 95 Knots and 110 knots when fully loaded depending on wind and air temperatures. The rate of climb needs to factor in the fuel load and weight, as it is all too easy to get into a stall by climbing too steeply on a fully loaded U-2. The climb speed should be about 160 knots to about 50,000 feet. Once a steady climb speed has been reached the aileron trim tabs need to be adjusted to alleviate any wing heavy loads to ensure the wings are not overstressed. As soon as any turbulent air is encountered the Gust control needs to be set to GUST. Once you reach an altitude of 65-70,000 feet, you can easily see the curvature of the earth through the canopy. Looking slightly up you can see the dark hue of outer space. At this height, you really do feel on top of the world and have no sensation of speed or the distance travelled using visual clues.

After several hours of flying, it is time to head back to base and prepare to land. It is the very fact that the U-2 loves to fly that makes landing so difficult. It is the most difficult aircraft I have ever had to land and is said to be the most difficult plane to land in the USAF.

It takes around 18 minutes to descend from 70,000 feet to 20,000 feet and you will cover around 100 nautical miles without any head or tail winds. Before descending you need to extend the speed brakes to ensure you do not overspeed, then lower the landing gear, pull the throttle back to almost idle and below 45,000 feet ensure the Gust control is set to 'GUST.' Finally, descend at around 160 Knots as this is the best speed to be at if you encounter any turbulence. As you reach about three miles out from the runway, you should be at about 1500 feet and flying about 30 Knots above stall speed. Final checks to ensure the landing gear is down and locked, flaps are set and the fuel balance is correct, also the gust control is set to 'FAIRED.' The final approach is conducted at about 750 feet and your speed is reduced to about 10 knots above stalling speed with flaps at full. You then allow the speed to drop to between 60-70 knots just before touching down, preferably with all four wheels at the same time. It all sounds very easy, but it is a very tricky and careful manoeuvre. As you must quite literally, stall the plane about two feet above the runway to get it to land. As the plane slows to its stall, the tail wheel lowers towards the runway and when the U-2 reaches a stall, the main wheel should then touch down. To a bystander, the landing looks very graceful, but from inside the cockpit it feels quite violent as you feel the plane stall and then struggle to keep the wings level. Once rolling along the runway you should then keep the wings off the runway for as long as possible and counteract the fact that they are still trying to lift the plane. As the plane finally begins to stop, you can allow one wing to touch the runway on its skid. Once stopped the ground crew re-install the pogos to make it much easier and safer to taxi back. Such is the fatigue, especially after a long flight, you need help getting out of the cockpit and your legs feel stiff for a short while afterwards. The best part for all pilots at the end of a mission or flight was getting out of the pressure suit before attending a debrief to discuss the mission and any technical issues encountered.

OPERATIONAL

With many pilots trained up to fly the U-2, they all wanted to become operational and conduct their first overflights. All the pilots had total faith in the plane and felt at the time that they were so high up they were invulnerable. President Eisenhower, however, was still prevaricating about whether to proceed or not. Only Two weeks earlier, the Soviet Union had protested a recently-completed series of overflights of northern Siberia by SAC RB-47s. These flights were flown out of Thule air base in Greenland and over the North Pole. Their objective was to map entry routes for SAC nuclear bombers and at the same time test Soviet air defences. For any overflights of Russia, the U-2s needed to be moved closer and the UK was initially looked at but Germany was favoured. There was a US air base at Wiesbaden near Frankfurt and the CIA had already used this base to conduct some covert low-level operations over Eastern Europe. All of us in Detachment A could be easily moved out there. The plan if the President gave his approval would be to conduct some flights over some of the satellite countries in Eastern Europe first.

If these were a success, then they could start to conduct overflights over Russia. We moved out to Wiesbaden on the 11 and 12 June 1956, which was a slight delay on the intended date. This was due to new engines needing to be shipped out, installed, and flight-tested. The CIA used the time to consult USAF on suitable targets. Finally, on the 20 June, Carl Overstreet climbed into his U-2 and made ready for an overflight of Eastern Europe. This was a high security mission and even at take-off, radio silence was maintained. All he got was a visual green light cue to say he could begin his take off. The route had been planned to avoid alerting the opposition's air defences. After take-off, he first flew west towards Belgium before turning back to overfly Wiesbaden and setting course for the east. Now at high altitude, he entered what was called 'denied territory' where the borders of East and West Germany and Czechoslovakia met. After passing north of Prague, he entered Poland, where it bordered East Germany and Czechoslovakia. If the aircraft was showing up on radar screens below, the hope was that the three satellite countries would have trouble co-ordinating their air defence reaction. Overstreet continued to Bydgoszcz before turning southeast to Warsaw and Lublin, then turning back to Kracow and Wroclaw. He flew directly over Prague as he headed southwest. As a further test of air defence radar co-ordination in NATO territory, the route took Overstreet all the way to the Rhine and the Franco-German border, before he made his descent for a safe landing at Wiesbaden.

The first overflight had been a total success. Bissell accompanied Edwin Land and the TCP chairman James Killian the next day to the White House for a briefing with President Eisenhower's military aide, Colonel Goodpaster. The President was in hospital for a stomach operation, but he had read the AQUATONE planning document. With the successful overflight of Eastern Europe, he was now inclined to permit a series of quick Soviet overflights to cover the highest-priority targets, but not until Chancellor Adenauer's agreement had been sought and obtained. Bissell then quickly flew to Bonn with CIA Deputy Director Pierre Cabell. Contrary to their fears, the 'Iron Chancellor' proved to be enthusiastic about the project. He thought it was a wonderful idea that must be carried out.

The photographs taken from the overflight of Eastern Europe were examined in detail. The camera that had been used was not the one intended for use in the U-2, as that was not ready. They had to make sure of an interim system designated the A-2. The A-2 comprised of three 24-inch focal length framing cameras taken from US Air Force stock, carefully overhauled, and improved with lenses personally polished by Dr Jim Baker. They had given excellent results, although there was also some less than good news regarding radar.

In the nose of the U-2 there was a small Electronic Intelligence (ELINT) receiver carried in the nose. The ELINT listened to radar activity in the S-band. Intelligence believed that the Warsaw Pact radar had no capability to detect targets flying above 60,000 feet. The U-2s system revealed that radar signals were being constantly received during the flight. This meant that the radar operators on the ground would have had radar echoes from the U-2 on their scopes as it flew within range of their sets. A further two U-2 missions were launched over satellite countries on the 2 July. They flew over five satellite countries reaching the Black Sea. The planes again performed faultlessly however, one of the A-2 camera rigs had problems and the photos were too blurry to be of any real use. Bisslle told Colonel Goodpaster that they were ready for Soviet overflights and duly requested permission for a ten-day operation of overflights over Russia. President Eisenhower agreed and approved the plan the next day. He did ask if the satellite flights had been tracked at all.

It was American Independence Day (4 July) 1956 that Pilot Hervey Stockman took off from Wiesdaden at 6am. It would be the first of five deep penetration missions into Soviet airspace over the next five days. Each mission lasted about 8 hours - each mission was a success as planes and cameras performed faultlessly. As each mission returned successfully, each pilot reported seeing Soviet fighters trying to intercept them. The U-2 had a periscope type view sight so the pilot could look down, and on every flight MiG fighters could be seen below. It became obvious, though they were being directed to a target the ground controllers could see and were too far below to pose any real threat to the U-2. This was further backed up when intercepted voice reports from the Soviet Air Defence, suggesting that the Soviet Air Defence was much better than had been thought. The next mission flew all the way to Moscow and obtained some excellent pictures of the first Soviet surface-to-air missile system. The West had glimpsed this unusual development along Moscow's outer ring road, but its status was unknown. As the U-2 passed over the site the pilot, Carmine Vito was lucky that none of the SA-1 missiles were kept at the site. Carmine and his U-2 had been picked up by an early warning radar at around 65,000 feet. Although the Soviet air defence experts discounted it, as they thought no aircraft could fly that high. Although as a precaution, the SA-1 missiles were moved to the launch site and installed ready to fire.

The third and fourth overflights were delayed by cloud cover over the target areas for a couple of days. It was decided to conduct the third and fourth overflights at the same time on 9 July 1956. The fifth flight was conducted on the 10 July and had not long landed at Wiesbaden, when a note was delivered to Washington, warning the Americans of their gross violation of Soviet airspace for reconnaissance reasons, by a twin-engine bomber that belonged to the US Air Force. The note further identified West Germany as the origin of the flights and described part of the route for the flights on the 4 and 5 July along with a complaint about a further intrusion on 9 July. The Soviets had identified the U-2 as the culprit, although their tracking was not perfect as they said they had tracked two flights on the 5 July when only one flight took place. President Eisenhower immediately halted the operation. The overflights had been a real technical breakthrough in a time before satellite imagery. In a memo by DPS Executive Officer Herb Miller:

"For the first time, we are really able to say that we understand much that was going on in the Soviet Union on 4 July 1956. We now have a cross-section of the entire Soviet way of life for that date - their military installations, their farms, their irrigation systems, their factories, their power systems to feed the factories, their housing for the people who run the factories, their recreation, their railroads and the amount of traffic they carry, their scientific accomplishment at least in the field of electronics, the port activities. These are but a few examples of the many things which tend to spell out the real intentions, objectives and qualities of the Soviet Union, which we must fully understand and appreciate if we are to be successful in negotiating a lasting peace for the world."

President Eisenhower was too concerned about the whole operation. Seeing enlargements of some of the dramatic photographs taken, did nothing to change his mind. The actual photographs taken revealed that the offensive firepower the Soviets had, had been overestimated. It was thought that at Soviet airfields they might find might find at least two regiments of heavy four-jet Myasischev M-4 bombers. Given the

NATO name the Bison, the first of these had been spotted three years earlier at the Fili airframe factory in a Moscow suburb. More had subsequently appeared over Moscow in staged flyovers. The Bison was thought to be capable of delivering a nuclear warhead to US territory and could pose a real threat. A second long-range bomber, the four-turboprop Bear, had also flown over Moscow. It took many months for the photo interpreters to work through the vast amount of imagery from the first five U-2 missions. It took until early 1957 to analyse it in full. The air power and the number of Bisons and Bears were much less than thought. These initial missions only captured a snapshot of what the Soviet capabilities were. Still left to be photographed were machine-building and other factories producing radio, radar and electronic equipment; design bureaus and research institutes, especially those identified with Soviet guided missile development; weapons storage sites, uranium mine in Estonia, Shipyards, transport infrastructure, ports and submarine bases including railroad junctions.

President Eisenhower still wanted a better relationship with the Soviet leadership and the overflights had done nothing to help the relationship. The Soviets saw the overflights as clear provocation and he was worried that the Soviets could see these as a precursor to a nuclear attack. This was the Cold War and tensions were high on both sides. The photographs taken so far had enabled the Air Force to add to its lists of targets with updated target locations, should a nuclear war ensue. Bissell and colleagues in the US intelligence community were deeply disappointed. There were still many high-priority targets to cover, such as Kapustin Yar and other known guided missile test ranges, atomic energy plants, tactical airfields. Some of these would best be allocated to another detachment (Detachment B) that was due to be deployed to Turkey. What had been found out was that Soviet radars in the southern region were as least as good as those in European Russia.

CHANGE OF PLANS

Richard Bissell now realised that avoiding detection was now the main problem for Project AQUATONE. During a meeting with Kelly Johnson and some of the other Boston scientists in mid-August 1956, a discussion took place about the possibility of adding radar-cancelling devices to the U-2. Ed Purcell explained his theories of how radar detection could be avoided, along with Frank Rodgers from MIT's Radiation Laboratory was recruited to apply them to the U-2. The Project would be called, project RAINBOW. This would be the first attempt at trying to make an operational aircraft stealthier.

Back in Germany an unexpected stimulus to U-2 operations came from Egypt as tensions rose after President Nasser nationalized the Suez Canal. We began flying missions from Germany over Egypt in late August, sometimes flying roundtrips from Wiesbaden, sometimes landing at Incirlik airbase in Turkey. Egypt, Jordan, Israel, the Lebanon, Syria and some North African countries were overflown. No permission to overfly had been sought and there was virtually no reaction from any of the air defences these countries had.

Detachment B was deployed to Incirlik in mid-August, and they took over all the flights in the Middle East by mid-October. Their frequency was stepped up as the UK, France and Israel put plans in place to invade and retake the Suez Canal. As the U-2 overflew Cyprus, Malta and French ports the British and French military build-up was captured on film. To speed up the process of interpreting all the photographs, CIA analysts were sent to the Air Force photo-processing and interpretation facility at Wiesbaden. Later, the CIA decided to set up its own temporary photo-interpretation facility at Adana.

All of Detachment A moved from Wiesbaden to the more isolated Giebelstadt airbase still in Germany in October 1956. At the time, we were still pretty much unemployed as Eastern Europe and Russia were still off-limits. President Eisenhower did approve some overflights of the southern satellite areas. We could fly three times over Albania, Bulgaria, Romania and Yugoslavia towards the end of 1956. The CIA was getting frustrated with the inability to be able to fully use the U-2.

The feeling was that the U-2 would become outdated before it had realised its full potential. It was hoped the RAINBOW project would save the U-2 from falling into disuse by making it less visible to radar. During the first half of 1957, several U-2s were coated with radar absorbing materials or fitted with radar deflecting wires that had already fooled some US radars. This new version of the U-2 was deployed to Detachment B and the newly formed Detachment C in Japan. However, during operational testing along the Soviet Border the S-band Tokens and the lower, VHF-band Soviet radars nicknamed Dumbo and Knife Rest, it was much more difficult to fool them. The additional weight of the various steal modifications also lowered the maximum height the U-2 could fly at by 5,000 feet. What US intelligence did realise, however, was that there were still some gaps in Soviet early-warning radar coverage. These gaps were over the remote Turkmen, Tadzhik and Kirgiz republics. The CIA went about gaining permission to launch U-2 overflights from Pakistan. In July 1957, President Eisenhower requested permission from Pakistan's Prime Minister Huseyn Suhrawardy for the U.S. to establish a secret intelligence facility in Pakistan and for the U-2 spy plane to fly from Pakistan. A series of missions was then approved by President Eisenhower. From 5 August 1957, for the next five weeks Detachment B flew deep into the Soviet Union nine times on Operation SOFT TOUCH. The operation targeted a number of high priority targets, which were photographed. This included the new Inter Continental Ballistic Missile (ICBM) test launch site at Tyuratam, along with a nuclear weapons development facilities as far north as Tomsk.

This flood of new U-2 photographs kept analysts busy for months. The CIA then planned for a new overflight campaign in spring 1958. On 1 March 1958 one of the stealthy U-2s took off from Japan to fly over the Soviet Far East. It was detected and intercepted by MiG fighters that came uncomfortably close. After the interception, the Soviets sent a new protest note to President Eisenhower, who immediately suspended U-2 flights over Russia again.

During the next 16 months, the President was still reluctant to authorise any more missions. His greatest concern was if a plane failed over Russia and the potential propaganda and embarrassment that could cause. The growing concern of the Soviet missile capability in the so called 'missile gap' led President Eisenhower to approve a few more Soviet overflights from July 1959. The US knew the Soviets had been testing ICBMs for the past two years at Tyuratam. They wanted to know if they had been secretly moved to other locations and what threat they proposed. The US at the time were also developing their own ICBMs.

These latest U-2 missions would also be launched from Pakistan as the Soviet early warning radar in the border areas was still not good enough to detect the U-2. Other Soviet radars could track the U-2 for short periods of time, but not long enough to run a risk on interception. This was to the U-2s favour as they had to fly over several the mobile SA-2 surface to air missile (SAM) batteries, which were much more capable than the SA-1 surface to air missiles. The SA-2 is a high-altitude, command guided SAM. Since its first deployment in 1957 it has become the most widely deployed air defence missile systems in history. It scored the first destruction of an enemy aircraft by a SAM, shooting down a Taiwanese Martin RB-57D Canberra over China, on October 7, 1959, by hitting it with three V-750 (1D) missiles at an altitude of 20 km (65,600ft). The success was attributed to Chinese MiG fighters, to keep the SA-2 program secret. Although US intelligence believed the SA-2 could only intercept up to 60,000 feet. With a new engine the U-2 was able to cruise at 70,000 feet once again and thought to be once again out of range of other aircraft or missiles.

Two proposed overflights that would cover the northern rail- road lines received the strongest consideration. Both plans contained new features. Operation TIME STEP called for a U-2 to take off from the USAF base at Thule, Greenland, which would be the first over- flight staged from this base. The aircraft would then fly over Novaya Zemlya on its way to cover the railroad lines from the Polyarnyy Ural Mountains to Kotlas. The return flight would be over Murmansk with the landing to take place at either Bodo or Andoya on Norway's northeast coast. The other would be the ill-fated operation GRAND SLAM flown by Garry Powers. Operation GRAND SLAM, was the first U-2 mission planned to fly over the whole of the Soviet Union. All previous missions had penetrated no more than halfway before exiting in the general direction from which they had entered. Operation GRAND SLAM proposed to fly across the Soviet Union from south to north, departing from Peshawar, Pakistan, and landing in Bodo, Norway. The mission would overtly Tyuratam, Sverdlovsk, Kirov, Koclas, Severodvinsk, and Murmansk. On 14 March 1960, Colonel Burke stated:

"Operation 'TIMESTEP is our last choice because we can assume, with a 90% probability of being correct, that we will be detected on entry, tracked accurately throughout the period in denied territory (approximately four hours), and will evoke a strong PVO (Soviet Air Defense) reaction. This flight plan would permit alerting of SAM sites. And pre-positioning of missile equipped fighters in the Murmansk area (point of exit) thus enhancing the possibility of successful intercept. In addition, we must assume that even were the Soviets unable to physically interfere with such an incursion. Sufficient evidence will be available to permit them to document a diplomatic protest should they desire to do."

GARY POWERS

Francis Gary Powers was born in Jenkins, Kentucky on 17 August 1929. He grew up in Pound, Virginia, just across the state border. He Graduated from Milligan College in Tennessee. Then in 1950, he was commissioned as a second lieutenant in the United States Air Force. After completing his training, Powers was assigned to the 468th Strategic Fighter Squadron at Turner Air Force Base, Georgia, as an F-84 Thunderjet pilot. Powers was discharged from the Air Force in 1956 with the rank of captain. He then joined the CIA's U-2 program at the civilian grade of GS-12. Sadly, Powers was killed in 1977, in a helicopter accident. He had been covering brush fires in Santa Barbara County and was returning home in a Bell 206 Jet Ranger when it ran out of fuel and crashed in the Sepulveda Dam Recreation Area several miles short of Burbank Airport. In his last heroic act, he steered the helicopter away from a group of children saving them.

Garry Powers took off from Peshawar airport on 1 May 1960, which was fifteen days before a scheduled opening of an East-West summit in Paris. Powers quickly got the U-2 up to its cruising height of 70,500 feet for the long overflight over Russia. The flight had been delayed several times due to bad weather over Russia. The operations code word was GRAND SLAM. Power's mission, was to overfly ICBM sites at the Baikonur Cosmodrome and Plesetsk Cosmodrome, before landing at Bodø in Norway. The Soviets, currently at the time, had six ICBM launch pads, four at Plesetsk and two at Baikonur. The other target was Mayak, then named Chelyabinsk-65, an important industrial centre of plutonium processing.

The Soviets had expected the flight and the whole of the Soviet Air Defence was on red alert from Central Asia, Kazakhstan, Siberia, Ural, to the U.S.S.R, European Region and Extreme North. It was not long before Powers U-2 had been detected by radar operators and Lieutenant General of the Air Force Yevgeniy Savitskiy ordered the air-unit commanders, *"to attack the violator by all alert flights located in the area of foreign plane's course, and to ram if necessary"*.

Soviet fighters were scrambled to intercept, but as per usual, they could not reach the height that the U-2 was flying at and were unable to intercept. There were several SAM sites that the U-2 would pass over, one failed to intercept due to not being on duty on that day. Finally, about 4 and half hours into the flight a SAM site in the Ural Region, could successfully fire a SAM which detonated just behind Power's U-2 causing it to start to disintegrate. It was one of three that had been fired as part of a salvo at the U-2.

The U-2 now spiralled down toward the ground and Powers looked for a way out. Unable to use the ejection seat because the centrifugal force had thrown him into the canopy. Powers released the canopy and prepared to bail out. He was waiting to arm the destruction device at the last minute, so that it would not go off while he was still in the plane. When he released his seatbelt. He was immediately sucked out of the aircraft and found himself dangling by his oxygen hose; unable to reach the destruction switches. Finally, the hose broke and he flew away from the falling aircraft. After he had fallen for several thousand feet, Powers parachute opened automatically. Powers drifted to earth, where he was quickly surrounded by farmers and then by Soviet officials. Powers could have used a lethal toxin to kill himself as per operation orders, but chose not to. The toxin was contained in a modified silver dollar, which itself contained a lethal, shellfish-derived saxitoxin-tipped needle. It took 30 minutes for the SA-2 SAM site to realise they had shot a U-2 down. They also found out that another missile from the salvo had hit and shot down a MiG-19 fighter being piloted by Sergei Safronov. America knew that they had lost a U-2 and immediately put a cover story in place via NASA. NASA released a very detailed press release noting that an aircraft had "gone missing" north of Turkey. The press release speculated that Powers might have lost consciousness whilst the autopilot was still engaged. They even went on to say 'falsely' that Powers had reported over the emergency radio frequency he was having oxygen difficulties. To further add credence to these claims, a U-2 was quickly painted in NASA colours and shown to the media. The CIA had assumed that Powers was dead and the U-2 had been destroyed. Therefore, they thought using NASA for a cover story was the best option available to them.

However, the wrong assessment had been made; Nikita Khrushchev used the American mistake to embarrass the US President along with his administration. When Nikita Khrushchev found out about the cover story that the Americans had released, he developed a cunning political trap for President Eisenhower. His plan began with the release of information to the world that a spy plane had been shot down in Soviet territory, but he did not reveal that the pilot of the aircraft had been recovered and was still alive. With the information that Nikita Khrushchev released, the Americans believed that they would be able to continue with their cover story that the crashed plane was a weather research aircraft and not a military spy plane. The American cover story stated that the U-2 had been flying over Turkey when the pilot ran into Oxygen difficulties. They then claimed that the plane had continued the same path due to its autopilot, and the plane that crashed could be the very same aircraft that they had lost. To then make the story seem even more realistic, all U-2s were grounded so that their oxygen systems could be checked. To ensure that no other U-2s would stray off course weather missions.

On 7 May, Khrushchev sprang his trap and announced to the world:

"I must tell you a secret. When I made my first report I deliberately did not say that the pilot was alive and well... and now just look how many silly things the Americans have said."

As the trap began to come together, it became clear that Gary Powers was alive and that he had told the Soviets about his mission. With the release of photographs, it was soon evident that much of the U-2s covert technologies had survived the crash and the Soviets knew exactly what the U-2 had been used for. This made it easy to reveal the cover story was a fabricated lie to cover up the truth. Upon his capture, Gary Powers had told his Soviet captors what his mission had been and why he had been in Soviet airspace. He did this because of orders that he had received before he went on his mission. Powers then under pressure pleaded guilty to espionage and was convicted on 19 August

1960. He was sentenced to three years' imprisonment and seven years of hard labour. In the end, Powers served one year and nine months of the sentence, before he was exchanged for Rudolf Abel on 10 February 1962. Abel was a Soviet intelligence officer that had been arrested on charges of conspiracy by FBI agents in 1957. A large part of the U-2 wreck along with items from Powers survival pack, is on still on display in the Central Armed Forces Museum in Moscow. A small part of the U-2 was also returned to America and is now on display in the National Cryptologic Museum.

The loss of Powers' U-2 ultimately resulted in the end of Detachment B in Turkey. As soon as the Development Projects Division teamed found out Powers was alive in Soviet hands, it immediately evacuated all the British pilots from Adana to ensure that their involvement in the project was kept secret. Project officials did hope that flights might resume eventually from Adana. However, this was unlikely with President Eisenhower's order ending overflights of the Soviet Union made this highly unlikely. Less than four weeks later. A coup ousted the government of Turkish Premier Adnan Menderes on the night of 27 May 1960. The new government had not been briefed on the U-2. This meant no flights could be authorised even ones to maintain the U-2s stationed their airworthiness. U-2s flew also unable to fly out of Adana. Instead of being ferried home, three of the four remaining U-2s were disassembled and loaded aboard C-124 cargo planes for the return trip to the United States.

CUBAN MISSILE CRISIS

With overflights of Russia stopped, the U-2 turned its attentions to Cuba. The United States was concerned about Communism and its expansion. A Latin American country allying openly with the USSR was regarded as unacceptable, given the Cold War background and high tensions between America and Russia. Such an ally would defy the Monroe Doctrine, a United States policy that, while limiting the United States involvement with European colonies and European affairs, held that European powers ought not to be involved with states in the Western Hemisphere. The Bay of Pigs invasion in April 1961 had been a disaster. This had been launched by President John F Kennedy, who replaced President Eisenhower at the end of his two terms in office in January 1961. It was President Eisenhower, who had put forward a plan for the overthrow of Fidel Castro and his administration to the US National Security Council (NSC). The Bay of Pigs plan was to train a counter revolutionary force and then send them to Cuba to help overthrow Castro. Over 1,400 paramilitaries, which were divided into five infantry battalions, along with one paratrooper battalion, assembled in Guatemala. On the 13 April 1961, they set off by boat for Cuba. On 15 April, eight CIA-supplied B-26 bombers attacked Cuban airfields and returned to the U.S. The main invasion landed at night on the 16 April, at a beach named Playa Girón in the Bay of Pigs. It initially overwhelmed the local revolutionary militia. The Cuban Army's counteroffensive was led by Captain José Ramón Fernández, before Castro decided to take personal control of the operation. On 20 April, the invaders finally surrendered, with most troops being publicly interrogated and then sent back to the United States.

The United States had been embarrassed publicly by the failed Bay of Pigs Invasion. What looked like a half-hearted invasion by the Soviets, left Soviet premier Nikita Khrushchev and his advisers with the impression that Kennedy was indecisive. One Soviet advisor writing, *"too young, intellectual, not prepared well for decision making in crisis situations, too intelligent and too weak."*

During the Berlin Crisis of 1961, Khrushchev's impression of Kennedy's weakness was further confirmed by the President's soft response, particularly the building of the Berlin Wall. When speaking to Soviet officials after the crisis, Khrushchev said, *I know for certain that Kennedy doesn't have a strong background, nor does he have the courage to stand up to a serious challenge."*

America was still working on plans the overthrow the Cuban government even after the failed Bay of Pigs operation. General Landsdale had described a plan called Operation MONGOOSE in January 1962, a secret program of terrorism against Cuba to remove the communists from power. In February 1962, America launched an embargo against Cuba. General Lansdale presented a top-secret 26-page timetable for putting in place plans for the overthrow of the Cuban Government, stating that guerrilla operations would begin in August and September, and in the first two weeks of October 1962.

After the US, had placed nuclear missiles in Turkey, aimed at Moscow, and the failed US attempt to overthrow the Cuban regime with the Bay of Pigs, and Operation Mongoose. Nikita Khrushchev proposed the idea of placing Soviet nuclear missiles on Cuba in May 1962, to deter any future invasion attempt. By 1962, the Soviets had only 20 ICBMs capable of delivering nuclear warheads to the United States from inside the Soviet Union. However, the poor reliability and accuracy of these missiles meant there was serious doubts about their effectiveness. A newer, more reliable generation of ICBMs would not be operational until at least 1965. This meant that in 1962 the Soviets had Medium Range Ballistic Missiles (MRBM) that could hit American Allies and Alaska from Russia, but not North America.

A group of Soviet military and missile construction specialists accompanied an agricultural delegation to Havana in early 1962. They had a meeting with Fidel Castro. The Cuban leadership still had a strong expectation that the US would invade Cuba again. The thought of installing nuclear missiles in Cuba was enthusiastically received. However, Fidel Castro was not happy about the missile deployment, as it could make Cuba look like a Soviet puppet. He was persuaded that having nuclear missiles in Cuba would be in the interests of the entire socialist camp.

Despite there being increasing amount of evidence that a military build was occurring in Cuba, no U-2 flights had been made over Cuba between the 5 September and 14 October. One reason for the pause was on August 30, when a U-2 operated by SAC Air Command flew over Sakhalin Island in the Soviet Far East by mistake. The Soviets lodged a protest and the US apologised. Then a Taiwanese-operated U-2 only nine days later, was lost over western China to a SAM thought to be an SA-2. America was worried that one of the Soviet SAMs in Cuba may shoot down a CIA U-2 creating another embarrassing international incident. It was decided to instead try the new Corona Satellite instead to gather intelligence. At the end of September 1962, US Navy reconnaissance aircraft photographed the Kasimov; a Soviet ship with large crates on its deck that appeared to be the size and shape of Il-28 light bombers. With this evidence and evidence from the Corona Satellite, it was felt it was now worth risking sending a U-2 in to investigate further. This time the flights were transferred to the US Air Force, as it was felt a cover story using the US Air Force would be better should another U-2 be shot down. The US first obtained U-2 photographic evidence of the missiles on 14 October 1962, when a U-2 flight piloted by Major Richard Heyser took pictures, of what turned out to be an SS-4 construction site at San Cristóbal, Pinar del Río Province, in western Cuba. Initiating the thirteen days of the Cuban Missile crisis, and the closest the world came to a nuclear war during the Cold War period. On 15 October, the CIA's National Photographic Interpretation Centre reviewed the U-2 photographs and identified objects that they interpreted as medium range ballistic missiles.

Missile surveillance photo

That evening, the CIA notified the Department of State. President Kennedy was notified the next morning and reviewed the photographs taken by the U-2. The American came up with a list of actions, which were:

Do nothing: American vulnerability to Soviet missiles was not new. Newly placed missiles in Cuba made little strategic difference in the military balance of power.

Diplomacy: Use diplomatic pressure to get the Soviet Union to remove the missiles.

Warning: Send a message to Castro to warn him of the grave danger he, and Cuba were in.

Blockade: Use the US Navy to block any missiles from arriving in Cuba.

Air strike: Use the US Air Force to attack all known missile sites.

Invasion: Full force invasion of Cuba and overthrow of Castro.

On 18 October, President Kennedy met with Soviet Minister of Foreign Affairs, Andrei Gromyko. He claimed that the weapons were for defensive purposes only. President Kennedy not wanting to panic the America public or expose what he already knew. Decided not to reveal he was already aware of a missile build up in Cuba. By 19 October, U-2 spy flights had been undertaken on a frequent basis and had shown four operational sites. On the 21 October, President

Kennedy decided a full-scale invasion was not their first option and initially a blockade would be the best first course of action. A blockade was, however, according to international law an act of war. However, the President felt that this alone would not provoke the Soviets into a full-scale war. Legal experts at the State Department and Justice Department thought that a declaration of war could be avoided so long as another legal justification, based on the Rio Treaty was put in place. The Rio Treaty was an agreement signed in 1947 in Rio de Janeiro, among many countries of America. The main principle the treaty contained in its articles was that an attack against one was to be considered an attack against them all.

On 20 October, President Kennedy departed for Washington for scheduled campaign speeches in Cleveland and the West Coast. At this point, the American public knew nothing about the events occurring in Cuba. Kennedy's Press Secretary announced on the same day, that the President is having to cancel the remainder of his campaign due to a respiratory infection, so that the President could be released to deal with the Cuban missile crisis. President Kennedy met with his advisors and ordered a defensive blockade be put in place as soon as possible. He also reviewed and then approved the operation. President Kennedy's television address to the American public was scheduled for the next evening.

On 21 October 1962 Kennedy is told by General Maxwell Taylor that an air strike could not guarantee destruction all Soviet missiles in Cuba. Kennedy decided on a blockade of Cuba for the time being. Kennedy also asked the press to respect that he has an element of surprise, as he is unsure of what the Soviets will do next. Another U-2 overflight of Cuba on 21 October that day revealed MiG fighter aircraft and Soviet bombers being rapidly assembled along with the construction of cruise missile site on Cuba's northern shore.

On 22 October, President Kennedy along with Congressional leaders assembled at the White House for a meeting. They were all shown the photographic evidence of the Soviet missile installations captured by the U-2 overflights. All of the congressional leaders expressed their support, with many of them wanting to take stronger action than President Kennedy proposed. In the evening of the 22 October, President Kennedy addressed the nation in a televised speech, announcing the presence of offensive missile sites in Cuba. At the same time, the US military state was moved to DEFCON 3. DEFECON 2 is the 'next step to nuclear war,' and DEFECON 1 is 'nuclear war is imminent.

On 23 October, President Kennedy orders six Vought F-8 Crusader fighters undertake low-level reconnaissance mission over Cuba. The Organization of American States (OAS) unanimously approves the quarantine against Cuba as per the Rio Treaty. By the end of 23 October, US ships had taken up position along the quarantine line, 800 miles from Cuba.

President Kennedy sent his Brother Robert Kennedy to the Soviet embassy to talk with Ambassador Dobrynin in the evening of the 23 October. At the same time, President Kennedy received a letter from Khrushchev, who stated there is a, *"serious threat to peace and security of peoples."* To try and placate things a little as well as give Khrushchev more time, President Kennedy pulls the blockade back to 500 miles.

On October 24 1962, Soviet ships travelling to Cuba containing a cargo of maybe military value, either slow down or turn around except for one ship. At the same time, US, military forces go to DEFCON 2.

On October 25, 1962 Kennedy sent a letter stating that the United States had been forced into action after receiving repeated assurances that no offensive missiles were being placed in Cuba, and that when these assurances proved to be false, the deployment, *"required the responses I have announced... I hope that your government will take necessary action to permit a restoration of the earlier situation."*

At the same time, EX-COMM discusses a proposal to withdraw US missiles from Turkey in exchange for the withdrawal of Soviet missiles in Cuba. To see if a peaceful resolution could resolve the situation.

On 26 October, the Soviet ship Marucla was cleared through the blockade. President Kennedy, during an EX-COMM meeting, says that he believes the blockade by itself alone cannot force the Soviet government to remove its missiles from Cuba. The CIA report back, was that work on the missile sites had continued and they were now attempting, to camouflage the missile sites. The KGB station chief in Washington, Aleksandr Fomin requests a meeting with ABC News correspondent John Scali. Aleksandr Fomin proposes the dismantling of Soviet bases in Cuba under U.N. supervision in exchange for a public pledge from the U.S. not to invade Cuba. Khrushchev reinforces this option by sending another letter to President Kennedy, stating that the Soviets would remove the missiles from Cuba if Kennedy would publicly announce never to invade Cuba.

On 27 October, Khrushchev sent another letter to President Kennedy, proposing a public trade of Soviet missiles in Cuba for US missiles in Turkey. In Cuba at approximately 12:00 pm EDT, whilst on an overflight mission, a U-2 was struck by a SA-2 SAM missile, launched from Cuba. The U-2 crashed, killing the pilot, Major Rudolf Anderson. The stress in negotiations between the Soviets and the US intensified. It was only much later, it was learned that the decision to fire the missile was made locally by a Soviet commander acting on his own authority. On the same day, a U-2 accidentally strayed into Soviet airspace near Alaska, very nearly being intercepted by Soviet fighters. A discussion about the removal of missiles from Cuba was finally made on 27 October between Ambassador Dobrynin and Robert Kennedy. President Kennedy wrote another letter Khrushchev stating that he will make a statement that the US will not invade Cuba if Khrushchev removes the missiles from Cuba.

On 28 October, Khrushchev announced over Radio Moscow, that he has agreed to remove the missiles from Cuba.

The compromise had embarrassed Khrushchev and the Soviet Union because the withdrawal of US missiles from Italy and Turkey was a secret deal between Kennedy and Khrushchev. The Soviets were retreating from circumstances that they had started. Khrushchev's fall from power two years later was in part because of the embarrassment caused by both Khrushchev's eventual concessions to the US and his ineptitude in precipitating the crisis in the first place. According to

Ambassador Dobrynin, the top Soviet leadership took the Cuban outcome *as "a blow to its prestige bordering on humiliation."*

Cuba saw the outcome as a partial betrayal by the Soviets, given that decisions on how to resolve the crisis had been made exclusively by Kennedy and Khrushchev. Castro was especially upset that certain issues of interest to Cuba, such as the status of the US Naval Base in Guantánamo, were not addressed. This caused Cuban-Soviet relations to deteriorate for years to come. On the other hand, Cuba continued to be protected from a US invasion.

Project OXCART

Even before the U-2 became operational in June 1956, CIA project officials had estimated that it had a life expectancy between 18 months and two years, for flying safely over the Soviet Union. Richard Bissell, by August 1965 had his concerns about the U-2s vulnerability and felt it would not be in service for more than six months. Project RAINBOW was trying to make the U-2 stealthier was brought about to extend its life. Project RAINBOW was cancelled in May 1958 after the Soviets were still able to track the U-2.

Even before project RAINBOW, Bissell and his Air Force assistant had started to look at a more radical solution to the problem of the Soviets being able to detect highflying aircraft. They visited several aircraft manufacturers in the summer of 1956 trying to look for new ideas. Northrop had the proposal for a large aircraft with a high lift wing and had been based around ideas they had gleaned from studying a captured German Horton bomber. The aircraft's wing would not be made of metal and constructed using a bridge type truss on the upper side of the wing to give rigidity. The aircraft would be able to achieve altitudes of 80,000 to 90,000 at subsonic speeds. As good as the design was, it did not solve the issue of radar detection and their thoughts moved to supersonic designs. In August 1957. The Scientific Engineering Institute (SEI). A CIA proprietary firm that had been working on ways to reduce the U-2's vulnerability to radar, also started to investigate if it was possible to design an aircraft with a very small radar cross section. SEI soon found out that when flying at supersonic speed it greatly reduced the chances of being detected by radar. With this new-found knowledge the CIA focused their attention on building an aircraft that could fly very fast and very high along with being as undetectable by radar as possible.

By the autumn of 1957, Bissell and his Air Force assistant had been able to collect quite allot of ideas for a successor to the U-2 that they needed to set up an advisory commission to assist in a selection process. A committee made up of scientists and engineers was thought to be the most useful method especially as the project would be an expensive one. Edwin Land was appointed as the new chairman of the committee. Scientists and engineers who had been advisors to other similar projects were placed on the committee. The first committee meeting was held in November 1957 with a further six meetings between July 1958 and August 1959. Along with scientists and engineers some aircraft designers also attended some of the meetings. Lockheed was one of the most prominent firms involved in the search for a new aircraft. Lockheed had the successful Convair and was building the B-58 supersonic bomber. The B-58 'Hustler' was the first operational supersonic jet bomber capable of Mach 2 flight. Lockheed was working with the air force on a faster B-58 called the B-58B 'Super Hustler' but cancelled due to budgetary considerations. Kelly Johnson had many lengthy discussions with Bissell on a successor for the U-2 and he began designing an aircraft that would cruise at Mach 3.0 at 90,000 feet and higher. Kelly Johnson presented his idea on 23 July 1958 to the advisory committee and they showed interest in Kelly Johnsons approach. At the same meeting, some representatives from the Navy also showed a concept of an inflatable vehicle powered by a rocket initially to get to a speed the ramjets could produce thrust. It would be lifted into the atmosphere by a large balloon. When the Navy supplied further calculations which Kelly Johnson looked at. He could quickly calculate that the size of the balloon needed to lift the vehicle would have to be about a mile in diameter and need a surface area of one-seventh of an acre.

Lockheed had looked at several possible configurations, some that were based on ramjet others with both ram-and turbojets. Personnel at Lockheed's Skunk Works referred to these aircraft concepts as 'Archangel 1' and 'Archangel 2 'so a carryover from the nickname of the U-2 which had been known as 'Angel.' Later these were cut down to A1 and A2

In September 1958, the committee met to look over all the proposals including the Navy one and one from Boeing for a 190 foot, hydrogen filled inflatable aircraft. Lockheed also had a design for a hydrogen-powered aircraft (the CL-400). The committee looked at two other designs by Kelly Johnson. One was subsonic aircraft with a very-low-radar cross section that did not have a tail and called the G2A and a new supersonic design called the A-2. The committee did not accept either of the designs. The G2A due to its low speed and the A-2 due to needing exotic fuels for its ramjets and the overall high cost of the design. The committee decided to approve the continuation of Convair's work on a ramjet-powered Mach 4.0 "parasite" aircraft that would be launched from a specially configured version of the B-58B bomber. The design called FISH was called a parasite, as it could not take off on its own and needed a mother aircraft to launch it from a higher altitude that was required so the ramjet engine could start. Two months later, after reviewing the Convair proposal and looking at yet another Lockheed design called the A-3. The committee felt that it would be feasible to build an aircraft whose speed and altitude would make radar tracking difficult or impossible. Funds were now required to approve more work on the project and allow for more studies and tests. On the 7 December 1958, President Eisenhower was briefed on the plans for a successor for the U-2. The President did support further progress of the project, but at the same time wanted to ensure that any procurement should not really occur on an untested aircraft. It was thought the US Air Force could transfer some reconnaissance money to support the project and wanted a further meeting when the next phase of work had been completed.

The next phase would see Lockheed and Convair battle it out. With funding for the proposed new type of aircraft now available, Bissell asked Lockheed and Convair to submit detailed proposals. During the first half of 1959, both Lockheed and Convair worked to reduce the radar cross section of their designs, with assistance from Franklin Rodgers of the Scientific Engineering Institute. Whilst pursuing his antiradar studies, Rodgers had discovered a phenomenon that he believed could be used to advantage by the new reconnaissance aircraft. It was known as the Blip/Scan Ratio, but also referred to as the Rodgers' Effect, this phenomenon involved three elements, the altitude of the object being illuminated by the radar, the strength of a radar return, and the persistence of the radar return on the radar screen. Nearly all tracking radars in the 1950s swept a band of sky 30 to 45 degrees and 360 degrees in circumference. An object that appeared in this band would reflect the radar pulse in a manner that was proportional to the size of the object it had picked up. Rogers determined that a high-altitude aircraft flying at high speed would return a much smaller blip on the radar screen if indeed it could be seen at all. For the phenomenon to work the aircraft must be flying at 90,000 feet and have a radar cross section of 10 square metres preferably not much over 5 square metres. To make such a small radar cross section the designers would have to make many concessions to both its aerodynamics and structural design.

By the summer of 1959, both firms had completed their proposals. In June 1959, Lockheed had submitted a design proposal for a ground-launched aircraft known as the A-11, it would have a speed of Mach a range of 3,200 miles, an altitude of 90,000 feet and a completion date of January 1961. Kelly Johnson had refused to reduce the aerodynamics of his to achieve a lower radar cross section, and even though the A-2's radar cross section, was not that great it was still larger than the smaller parasite aircraft being designed by Convair.

Lockheed continued to work on developing a design that would be harder to detect by radar. Convair received a new CIA contract to design an air-breathing twin-engine aircraft that would meet the general specifications. Then, following recommendations by the Land Committee, both Lockheed and Convair incorporated the Pratt & Whitney J58 power plant into their designs. This J58 had originally been developed for the Navy's large jet-powered flying boat, the Glenn L Martin Company's P6M Seamaster, and was the most powerful engine available. The J58 was a single-spool turbojet engine with an afterburner, producing produced 32,000lbf of thrust. It was the first engine that was designed to use an afterburner for an extended period. In 1958, the Navy had cancelled the Seamaster program, which had left Pratt & Whitney without a buyer for the powerful J58 engine. The Land committee had still not found a suitable design, but felt they were making good progress. A satellite capable of taking photographs was coming up against significant problems and President Eisenhower gave his final approval for a high-speed reconnaissance aircraft.

By the late summer of 1959, both Convair and Lockheed had completed new designs for a follow-on to the U-2. Convair had a new entry called KINGFISH and borrowed technology used in the F-102, F-106 B-58. It had a honeycomb construction with a crew escape capsule and two J58 engines on either wing. The radar cross section had been reduced further; extra features such as fibreglass inlet nozzles ceramic leading edges and wings all helped. Lockheed had also been busy preparing a new design and now called the A-12. It also made use of two J58 engines. The major contribution to reducing the radar cross section, was the addition of a cesium additive to the jet fuel. This reduced the cross section of the afterburner plume. Lockheed had not come up with it themselves, as the original recommendation came from Edward Purcell of the Land committee. To withstand the heat of high-speed flight, Kelly Johnson proposed to build the A-12 out of Titanium, which would need new fabrication methods.

These two final proposals from Convair and Lockheed were submitted on 20 August 1959. Both designs had similar specifications with Lockheed having slightly better specifications in each category. Both could fly at a proposed Mack 3.2 but the A-12 had greater range and could cruise slightly higher. The A-12 also came in cheaper at $96.6 million compared to the KINGFISH at $121.6 million for twelve aircraft. In terms of radar detection, the Convair design was superior. Its smaller size and internally mounted engines gave it a smaller radar cross section than the Lockheed A-12. Some of the panel felt the KINGFISH was the better proposal. However, the Air Force convinced them otherwise due to existing cost overruns and issues with the existing B-58 program. Lockheed had just produced the U-2 under budget and on time. Lockheed also had experience of running a highly secretive program with the U-2. There were still concerns over the Lockheed's radar cross section. Lockheed had until 1 January 1960 to reduce it and was awarded a four-month contract on 14 September

1959 for antiradar studies to be conducted. The Cobra like appearance of the A-12 came from Edward Purcell and Franklin Rodgers theory that a continuously curving airframe would be difficult to track. It took 18 months in total to get an acceptable radar cross section, with a mock up A-12 was placed on a pylon and various radar scans undertaken, before more adjustments were made, until the target cross section was reached.

OXCART Development

The specification for the A-12 OXCART aircraft, stated it would achieve a speed of Mach 3.2, which would make it faster than a rifle bullet, and have a range of 4.120 nautical miles. It would reach altitudes of 84,500 to 97,600 feet. The A-12 would fly at five times the speed and nearly 3 miles higher than the U-2. The technological issues to fly at those speeds were huge. At Mach 3.2, the friction from the air would cause sections of the A-12s fuselage to heat up to 900F. All fluids such as hydraulic fluid, lubricants and fuel would need to operate safely at high temperatures as well. Such fluids had yet to be invented. Synthetic lubricants were one thing that was born out of the OXCART project. Even hydraulic pumps that could operate under such harsh conditions was not easy to overcome. The extreme height and high temperature issues meant using new materials to construct the airframe.

After the evaluation of many materials, Kelly Johnson chose titanium alloy (B-120) which has the properties of great strength, lightweight, weighing half that of stainless steel and good resistance to high temperatures. However, it is a costly metal and difficult to work with. As much as 80% of the early Titanium sourced was rejected on quality grounds. Once Lockheed had sufficient good quality Titanium, they had to fabricate new tools to work with it. As the traditional tools were too soft to work with the very hard titanium alloy. This also meant that traditional assembly line production would not be possible, adding to the cost of manufacture and pushing it over the original estimate. The pilot would also need to be protected from the high altitudes and heat. Instead of insulating the cockpit. Kelly Johnson decided that the pilot would wear a spacesuit with its own cooling and pressure control, as this would also help save weight as well as cost. OXCART pushed aviation technology to its limits and beyond. At the same time, many new aviation technologies were invented and our understanding of high speed, high altitude flight further enhanced.

Even the cameras that were to be fitted to the A-12 would pose a unique set of problems for their designers. Three different camera systems were developed, these cameras would provide a range of photography from high-ground-resolution stereo images of extremely-high-resolution images.

The Perkin-Elmer (P-E) entry, known as the Type-I camera was a high-ground-resolution general stereo camera using an f/4.0 I 8-inch lens and 6.6-inch film. It produced pairs of photographs covering a swath 71 miles wide with an approximately 30-percent stereo overlap. The system had a 5,000-foot film supply and could resolve 140 lines per millimetre and provide a ground resolution of 11 inches.

Eastman Kodak's design was called the Type-II was a high convergent stereo device with a 21-inch lens and 8-inch film. It could produce pairs of pictures which covered a swath of land of some 60 miles wide with a 30-percent overlap. It also had an 8,400-foot film with a resolution of 105 lines per millimetre and provide a ground resolution of 17 inches. The Hycon entry, designed by James Baker and known as the camera, was a camera with very high resolution. It was an advanced version of the B camera developed for the original U~2 program. It used a 48~inch t/5.6 lens to focus onto 9.5~inch film. Like the B camera, it could provide seven frames of photography covering a swath 41 miles wide with stereo overlap on 19 miles of the swath. The Hycon camera carried the largest film supply of the three cameras at 12,000 feet It could resolve 100 lines per millimetre and provide a ground resolution of 8 inches.

Each of the three camera systems had unique capabilities and advantages, so all three were purchased for the project. Before they could be employed in the aircraft. A different type of camera windows was needed. The A-12s camera window had to be completely free from optical distortion. Achieving this goal was difficult in a window whose exterior would be subjected to temperatures of 550F while the interior surface could only be only 15F. After three years and the expenditure of $52 million in research and development, producing the Corning Glass Works. Which had joined the effort as a Perkin-Elmer subcontractor. They solved the problem of a camera window that could withstand tremendous heat differentials. Its window was fused to the metal frame by a process involving sound waves.

Along with cameras, pilots would also be needed for the very unique and highly secretive A-12. These pilots would need to have a vast amount of experience and be extremely competent. All the pilots would come from the Air Force and they would have to be qualified in the most advanced fighters, be emotionally stable and well-motivated. The Air Force designed personnel and cover procedures so that with OXCART, both regular and reserve officers could volunteer. The A-12 cockpit had a size limitation like the U-2. All pilots had to be less than six feet tall and weigh less than 175 pounds. Once extensive physical and psychological tests had been conducted. Sixteen were selected for intensive security and medical screening by the Agency. By the end of this screening in November 1961, only five individuals had been approved and had accepted the Agency's offer of employment on a highly-classified project flying an extremely advanced aircraft. A second search and screening raised the number of pilots for OXCART to eleven. The thorough screening process produced an elite group of pilots; all but one of these eleven officers went on to become generals. The new pilots transferred from military to civilian status and received compensation and insurance arrangements somewhat better than those that had flown the U-2 had received.

The final area for development was a suitable and very secret test site for the actual aircraft to fly from. Over ten different airbases were looked at, that were due to close. However, in the end Area 51 was deemed to be the most secret and best location to test such a secret aircraft. Richard Bissell decided to upgrade the facilities, as the runway and other facilities were inadequate to take the OXCART project. A new 8,500-foot runway was completed by 15 November 1960. Kelly Johnson had been reluctant to have a standard Air Force runway with usual expansion joints every 25 feet because he feared this may well set up undesirable vibrations in the aircraft. At his suggestion, a 150-foot wide runway was constructed with six 25-foot-wide longitudinal sections, each 150 feet long but staggered. This layout put most of the expansion joints parallel to the direction of aircraft roll and reduced the frequency of the joints. Other improvements to Area 51 included the resurfacing of 18 miles of highway leading to the base so heavy fuel tankers could bring in fuel. Extra buildings for accommodation along with three additional hangars, which all came from the +Navy, were also erected.

The actual building of the A-12 was running behind schedule due to delays in the Titanium and the J58 engines. The delay on the engines was such, that Kelly Johnson began testing without the J58 engines by using Pratt & Whitney J75 engines, designed for the F-106 and would allow the A-12 to fly up to 50,000 feet at Mach 1.2. The first A-12 had to be adjusted slightly to fit the J75 engine. To keep costs from spiralling out of control, the original A-12 order was reduced from 12 to 10 for a total cost of $161 million. The cancelled A-12s was then later offset by the Air Force ordering a supersonic interceptor variant of the A-12 as a replacement for the F-108A Rapier project. The F-108 was to have was to have been a long-range, high-speed interceptor aircraft. It was cancelled in late 1960, due to a shortage of funds and the Soviet's adoption of ballistic missiles, having got no further than a wooden mock up. With the assistance of the Agency's west coast contracting office, the Air Force entered into an agreement with Lockheed to produce three AF-12 aircraft, based on the A- 12 design but modified to carry a second crew member and three air-to-air missiles. The project was called KEDLOCK, originally known as the AF-12 and changed later to the YF-12A. As with the F-108 it was designed to intercept enemy bombers long before they reached the United States. The Air Force had plans for a force of up to 100 YF-12As. In the end, only three YF-12As were delivered during 1963-1964. It was later cancelled by McNamara the Secretary of Defence at the time, as a cost cutting measure.

DELIVERY AND TESTING OF THE A-12

The first A-12, known as article 121, was assembled and tested at Burbank during January and February 1962. As it could not be flown to Area 51, the aircraft had to be partially disassembled and put on a specially designed trailer that cost nearly $100,000. The aircraft had to be completely concealed, which meant a crate that would cover a load 35 feet wide and 105 feet in length. With such a wide load, various trees and roadbanks had to be levelled. It was a two-day journey with the first A-12 arriving at Area 51 on 26 February 1962.

Once the fuselage had arrived at Area 51, it had its wings attached. Although it was then found that whilst putting fuel on board, the fuel was leaking out from the fuel tanks. This was due to the airframe being designed to be a 'loose' fit, so that at high speeds and the airframe being at 500F the expansion joints would narrow. The joins were filled with a pliable sealant; however, the jet fuel softened the sealant and caused 68 leaks to develop. They renewed all the sealant and it did reduce the leaks. It took some 30-54 hours to replace all the sealant due to the different curing temperatures required. The leaks were never fully sorted and the A-12 was given only enough fuel to get airborne, before being refuelled mid-air. A suitable sealant that would not be softened by the special jet fuel and withstand high temperatures was never found or developed.

On 25 April 1962, test pilot Louis Schalk took article 121, the first A-12 for an unofficial unannounced flight, which was an old Lockheed tradition. He flew the aircraft for less than two miles at an altitude of about 20 feet. He encountered considerable problems because of the improper hookup of several controls. These were promptly repaired and on 26 April. Schalk made the official maiden flight. After a perfect takeoff, the aircraft began shedding the triangular fillers that covered the frame- work of the chines along the edge of the aircraft body. The triangle fillets had been secured to the airframe with epoxy resin. These then had to be reaffixed to the aircraft, which took the next four days. Once the fillets were in place, the OXCART's official first flight took place on 30 April 1962, witnessed by a number of Agency personnel.

Richard Bissell was also present even though he had resigned from the agency. The official first flight was also the first flight with the wheels up. Piloted again by Schalk, OXCART took off at 70 knots and climbed to 30.000 feet. During the 59-minute flight, the A-12 achieved a top speed of 340 knots. Kelly Johnson declared it to be the smoothest first test flight of any aircraft he had designed and tested so far. On 2 May 1962, during the second test flight, OXCART broke the sound barrier, achieving a speed of Mach 1.1. Another four aircraft along with a two-seat trainer arrived at Area 51 before the end of 1962. On one delivery of an A-12 on 26 June 1962, one of the trucks carrying an A-12 hit a Greyhound bus travelling in the opposite direction. A payment of $4,890 was quickly dispatched to the bus company to pay for repairs. If it ended up in court, questions would be asked as to why the load the truck was carrying was so wide. Keeping the A-12 a secret would be hard as it was with the U-2. Air traffic controllers would soon see the aircraft on their scopes. To help keep the A-12 secret the Federal Aviation Administrator Najeeb E. Halaby was told about the A-12 and asked to help keep it secret. He briefed all his FAA regional chiefs on how to handle reports of unusually fast high-flying aircraft. Air controllers were told not to broadcast any sightings over the radio, but to put it in writing about their sightings and tracking of the A-12. The Air Force also gave a similar briefing to, the North American Air Defense Command (NORAD).

The initial flight tests could not explore the aircraft's full potential, due to the lack of J58 engines. Engine development was taking much longer than planned. Most of this could be attributed to the speed that the engine was required to operate at. It had to give never seen before performance levels at high speed and high temperatures. It took until January 1963 for the first ten engines to be delivered to Area 51. It was not until the 15 January 1963, that the first A-12 equipped with the J58 engine took to the skies. Testing continued, but as the speeds rose so did the problems with the engines. The first problems were encountered between Mach 2.4 and 2.8, due to the aircrafts shockwave interfering with the airflow to the engines. It was only by lengthy testing and design a new air inlet was designed that solved that problem. The new air inlet, had projection at the front-known as the spike. It was designed to move in or out as much as three feet to capture and contain the shock wave produced by the aircraft at high speed. This stopped the shockwave from entering the engine and disturbing the airflow into the engine.

Another issue early on was Foreign Object Damage (FOD), as the J58s gulped in air at such a rate they were in effect giant vacuum cleaners. The FOD damage, was caused when small objects from pens, bolts to metal shavings had fallen into the engine during construction of the aircraft. This then caused damage to the compressor blades and impeller during testing at Area 51. FOD damage from runway debris was another issue, necessitating the need for Area 51 staff to sweep the runway before every A-12 take-off. Testing for the A-12 continued when on the 24 May 1963, the first crash of an A-12 occurred. The pilot had decided to eject after receiving an erroneous and confusing airspeed indication. The aircraft was destroyed in the process, but the pilot was unhurt. A cover story of an F-105 having crashed was released to the press. All A-12s were subsequently grounded, whilst an investigation took place. In the end, ice in the Pitot tube that measured the air speed was found to be the cause of the issue. Another two A-12s were lost, on 12 July 1964, one crashed on landing when its pitch control servo froze, causing the aircraft to roll into a wing down position. The pilot ejected sideways from an altitude of 120 feet, his parachute opened and landed unhurt. Then on 28 December 1965, an A-12 crashed after takeoff because of an improperly wired stability augmentation system. The pilot was able to eject safely and it was found the accident had been caused by negligence due to incorrect wiring.

The A-12 made its first long-range, high-speed flight on 27 January 1965. The flight in total lasted 100 minutes. 75 minutes of the flight were flown at speeds of Mach 3.1 and more. The aircraft covered 2.580 miles at altitudes between 75,600 and 80,000 feet. The A-12 was performing well. The engine inlet, camera, hydraulic, navigation, and flight-control systems were all working extremely reliably. By 20 November 1965, the final validation flights for OXCART deployment were finished. During these tests, the A-12 achieved a maximum speed of Mach 3.29 an altitude of 90,000 feet, and sustained flight time above Mach 3.2 of 74 minutes. The maximum endurance test lasted six hours and 20 minutes. On 22 November, Kelly Johnson wrote to Brig. Gen. Jack C. Ledford. head of the Office of Special Activities, stating. *"The time has come when the bird should leave its nest."*

Three years and seven months after its first flight in April 1962, the A-12 was ready for operational use. All it required was some work for the most advanced aircraft ever built.

As the A-12 began to fly for longer periods at high speeds and altitudes, new problems arose. The most serious of these problems encountered was the aircraft's wiring. Continuing malfunctions of the inlet controls, communications equipment, ECM systems, and cockpit instruments were often attributable to wiring failures. Various wiring connectors and components had to withstand temperatures above 800F, along with structural flexing, vibration, and shock. These extremes were more than some of the materials could withstand and led to failure. Although officials blamed poor maintenance practice by Lockheed for the failures.

As the funding for the OXCART version for the Air Force increased dramatically, the Defense Department became concerned that it was unable to offer an explanation to the public for these expenditures. The Agency and Defense Department officials also recognised the growing danger that a crash or sightings of test flights could compromise the program. This led to an idea to reveal the Air Force's interceptor version of the A-12 to provide a cover for any OXCART sightings or crashes. It would also explain Air Force spending and help keep the journalists who had become aware of the aircraft's existence happy. It was decided to keep OXCART a secret, after a discussion with President Kennedy. Although those who wanted to reveal the Air Force version continued to campaign, especially as the testing of the aircraft was gathering valuable data that could be used to support other projects such as the B-70 bomber and for the SST program of building a supersonic airliner to compete with the United Kingdom and France with their Concord. The battle to reveal the aircraft continued after the assassination of President Kennedy and President Lyndon Johnson coming to office. Russia's latest radar TALLINN would be able to see the A-12 even with its low radar cross section, further adding an argument to reveal the YF-12. The final decision on the issue of revealing OXCART, came at a National Security Council meeting on 29 February 1964, when the decision to reveal the aircraft was made. President Johnson then held a news conference on the same day, at which he announced the successful development of an "advanced experimental jet aircraft, the A-11" which has been tested in sustained flight at more than 2,000 miles per hour and at altitudes more than 70,000 feet. President Johnson had spoken about the A-11 rather than the A-12. The aircraft that was revealed to the public was the Air Force's YF-12A, which had now been cancelled. Two YF-12s were flown to Edwards Air Force base, where they stayed to draw attention away from Area 51 where higher altitude and higher speed tests were now being undertaken with the A-12.

The process of revealing or surfacing versions of the OXCART continued, when on 25 July 1964, President Johnson revealed the existence of a new Air Force reconnaissance aircraft, which he called the SR-71 by mistake. He was supposed to say RS-71 the RS meaning Reconnaissance Strike. Although this version is conflicted by LeMay, who lobbied to modify Johnson's speech to read SR-71 instead of RS-7. In the end, it was decided it would be easier to change the name than correct the Presidents mistake and so the SR-71 the successor to the A-12 was born in name.

THE FUTURE OF THE A-12

With overflights of Soviet Union appearing to be out of the question, the A-12s eventual employment elsewhere in the world remained a strong possibility, particularly after the Cuban Missile Crisis of October 1962, had shown the need for manned reconnaissance aircraft. This had been boosted, as satellites had not been able to supply the kinds of coverage needed, U-2s had carried out numerous overflights of Cuba. The U-2 however, was vulnerable to SAMs and it was proven again, when one was shot down during the Cuban missile crisis. It had been thought to send an A-12 without its J58 engines over Cuba, but due to the potential of it being shot down and not fully flight tested this was felt to be far too risky. The U-2s continued to monitor the withdrawal of the missiles using the U-2 and could do so as a monitoring function without interference. However, the U-2 would be vulnerable if Russia decided to reintroduce ballistic missiles into Cuba. Such fears became even more heightened in the summer of 1964 after Soviet Premier Nikita Khrushchev told foreign visitors, one who was a columnist, Drew Pearson a former Senator William Benton, and Danish Prime Minister Jens Otto Krag that once the US elections had been held in November, U-2s flying over Cuba would be shot down. Attention was then turned towards the OXCART program to continue overflights over Cuba. The aircraft was not ready, but it was to be made emergency operational ready by 5 November. Although this deadline passed without any hostilities from Russia or Cuba. U-2s continued to fly missions with the A-12s held back for an emergency.

When the Agency declared that the A-12 had achieved emergency operational status, the A-12 however, was not prepared for electronic warfare. Only one of the several planned electronic countermeasure devices (ECM) had been installed into the A-12. It was still thought however, the A-12 could conduct overflights at a senior level. One issue with fitting ECM equipment was that should an A-12 be lost over enemy territory could compromise the same equipment used in other US fighters and bombers. These concerns led to a different approach to antiradar efforts. Project KEMPSTER tried to develop electron guns that could be mounted on the A-12 to generate an ion cloud that would reduce its radar visibility. After the loss of four U-2s over China along with the loss of numerous Air Force reconnaissance drones; preparations began to get the A-12 ready to operate over China, should the case be required and the President authorised such overflights.

Project BLACK SHIELD was the name given to the plan for Far East operations. The project called for A-12 aircraft based at Kadena air base on Okinawa. Three A-12s would be flown out there for 60 day periods, twice a year. Later there would be a permanent detachment based at Kadena. The base needed extra support facilities and real-time secure communications – which were installed by autumn 1965.

In the summer of 1965, after the United States had begun deploying large numbers of troops into South Vietnam. Southeast Asia became another possible target for the A-12. The continued use of U-2s for reconnaissance missions over North Vietnam was threatened by the deployment of Soviet-made SAMs. McNamara asked the CIA on 3 June 1965, whether the A-12 could replace the U-2. He was told that the A-12 could; now that it had passed its final operational tests.

Deployment of the A-12 was still something that the 303 committee had failed to agree on five separate occasions. The CIA then proposed using the A-12 for an overflight of Cuba to test the aircraft's ECM systems in a hostile environment. On 15 September, the 303 Committee considered and rejected this idea because sending the A-12 over Cuba would disturb the existing calm prevailing in that area of US foreign affairs.

With operational missions still ruled out, proficiency training remained the main order of business for the A-12 and its pilots. This led to improvements in mission plans and flight tactics that enabled the detachment to reduce the time required to deploy to Okinawa from 21 days to 15. Records continued to fall to the A-12. On 21 December 1966. A Lockheed test pilot flew an A-12 for 10,195 miles over the continental United States in slightly more than six hours, for an average speed of 1,659 miles per hour, which included inflight refuelling at speeds as low as 602 miles per hour. This flight set a record for speed and distance unapproachable by any other aircraft type.

Then Two weeks later, on 5 January 1967, an A-12 crashed after a fuel gauge malfunctioned and the aircraft ran out of fuel just short of the runway. The Pilot ejected, but was killed when he could not separate from his ejection seat. The press was told an SR-71 was missing and presumed to have gone down in the Nevada desert.

Missions to test the new Russian radar system called Tallinn were still being considered, as several potential missions had been turned down to avoid any potential political embarrassment. The A-12 could be used to collect tactical rather than strategic intelligence. The concern was the possibility of undetected SAMs that had been introduced into North Vietnam. President Johnson asked for a proposal to find these SAMs and the CIA suggested using the A-12. This got the President's approval and operation BLACK SHEILLD into the Far East was put into effect.

Equipment and personnel were shipped over to Kadena from 17 May 1967 and then on 22 May the first A-12 flew nonstop from Area 51 to Kadena with a flight time of six hours and six minutes. A second A-12 arrived on 24 May and the third and final A-12 left Area 51 on the 24 May 1967. Although a technical problem with the inertial navigation system meant it had to make a landing at Wake Island as a precautionary measure. The fault was corrected and the A-12 completed its journey to Kadena. It was the 31 May 1967 that the first operational mission was undertaken.

As the take-off time approached, Kadena was deluged by rain, but since weather over the area was clear. Flight preparations continued even though the A-12 had never operated in heavy rain taxied and took off from Kadena without incident. The A-12 was to fly over North Vietnam and then the demilitarized zone (DMZ). The mission was flown at Mach 3.1 and 80,000 feet, lasting 3 hours and 39 minutes. The A-12 managed to photograph some 70 out of the 190 known SAM sites, along with nine other priority targets over North Vietnam. The A-12s ECM did not detect any radar activity - which indicated the flight had gone unnoticed by the North Vietnamese and Chinese. A typical mission over North Vietnam required refuelling south of Okinawa, shortly after take-off due to the issues of fuel leaking on the ground. After the planned photos, had been taken it was time for a second aerial refuelling in the Thailand area before returning to Kadena. The A-12s speed meant that it only spent around 12 minutes over Vietnam in a single pass. When making a return pass it took 86 miles for the A-12 to complete the turn, which meant the A-12 occasionally passed into Chinese airspace. Once the A-12 had landed, the camera film was removed and then sent back to the US for processing. On later missions, the processing was done in a laboratory in Japan, so that US commanders in Vietnam could have the intelligence within 24 hours of the mission's completion.

Over the next six weeks, there were alerts for 15 BLACK SHIELD missions, seven of which were actually flown. Out of those seven missions, only four detected hostile radar signals. By mid-July 1967, BLACK SHIELD missions had provided sufficient evidence for analysts to conclude that no surface-to-surface missiles had been deployed in North Vietnam.

BLACK SHIELD continued unabated during the second half of 1967. From 16 to 31 December 1967, 26 missions were alerted and 15 were flown. On 17 September, one SAM tracked the A-12 with its accusation radar, but was unable to lock on to the A-12. The first missile to be fired at the A-12 was on 28 October and the missile contrails were captured on film. The ECM did their bit and the missile, posed no threat to the aircraft.

The only time the enemy came close to downing an A-12 was on 30 October 1967. Dennis Sullivan was on his first pass over North Vietnam when he detected he was being tracked by radar. Two SAM sites prepared to launch missiles but neither did. During Sullivan's second pass the North Vietnamese fired at least six missiles at the A-12, each missile confirmed by vapor trails on mission photography. The pilot saw these vapour trails and witnessed three missile detonations near but behind the A-12, which was travelling at Mach 3.1

at about 84,000 feet. On inspection of the aircraft after it had landed, revealed that a piece of metal had penetrated the underside of the right wing, passing through three layers of titanium, before becoming lodged against a support structure of the wing tank. The debris had obviously come from a missile detonation.

Due to budget concerns and the forthcoming SR-71, the A-12 program had ended on 28 December 1966, before operation BLACK SHEILD had begun in 1967.

The 29th and final mission over North Korea for the A-12 was flown by Ronald L. Layton on 8 May 1968. The final A-12 flight was made by Frank Murray on 21 June 1968, flying to the Palmdale, California storage facility. All A-12s were stored at Palmdale for nearly 20 years before being sent to various US museums.

The A-12 did not outlast the U-2, the aircraft it was supposed to replace. The A-12 lacked the quick-response capability of the U-2. A U-2 unit could be activated overnight and within a week, it could deploy abroad. Flying sorties and then return to home base. The A-12 required precise logistic planning for fuel and emergency landing and their inertial guidance systems needed several days for programming and stabilisation. Aerial tankers had to be deployed in advance along an A-12s flight path and provisioned with the highly-specialised fuel used by the J58 engines needed to run at high speed and altitude. All of this required a great deal of time and the effort of several hundred people. A U-2 mission could be planned and flown with a third fewer personnel, making it much more cost effective to both run and maintain and a major reason the U-2 is still flying today. Satellite technology had begun to replace the A-12 even before it had got off the ground, adding another nail to its coffin and reason for its demise.

SR-71

Air Force orders for variants of the CIA's A-12- the YF-12A interceptor and the SR-71 reconnaissance aircraft- had helped lower development and procurement costs for the original A-12. Nevertheless, once the Air Force had built up its own fleet of reconnaissance aircraft, budgetary experts began to criticise the existence of two expensive fleets of similar aircraft. In November 1965, the very month that the A-12 had been declared operational the Bureau of the Budget circulated a memorandum that expressed concern about the costs of the A-12 and SR-71 programs. It questioned both the total number of planes required for the combined fleets, and the necessity for a separate CIA fleet. The memorandum recommended phasing out the A-12 program by September 1966 and stopping any further procurement of the SR-71 models.

In the Bureau of the Budget, a study group was established to look for ways to reduce the cost of the A-12 and SR-71 programs. The study group consisted of C. W. Fischer from the Bureau of the Budget. Herbert Bennington from the Department of Defense, and John Parangoky from CIA. The study group listed three choices of action. The first was to maintain both fleets. The second to mothball the A-12s but share the SR-71 s between CIA and the Air Force and the third mothball the A-12s and assign all missions to Air Force SR-71

On 12 December 1966, four high level officials met to consider these alternatives. Over the objections of Helms, the other three officials decided to terminate the A-12 fleet. Concerned that this recommendation would strip the CIA of its supersonic reconnaissance capability, Helms then asked for the second option, that the SR-71 fleet was shared between CIA and the Air Force. One of the main issues was of the concern that the SR-71 was inferior to the SR-71. The SR-71 could not match the photographic coverage of the A-12, nor could the SR-71 fly as high. The Air Force maintained that its two-seat SR-71 had a better suite of sensors, with three different cameras, infrared detectors, aerial and EUNT-collection gear. Even when pitched against each other the A-12 and SR-71 proved to be just as good at taking photographs.

The decision to phase out the A-12 meant that the CIA had to develop a schedule for an orderly phase out of the A·l2. This activity was known as Project SCOPE COTTON. Project headquarters informed Deputy Secretary of Defense, Cyrus Vance on 10 January 1967 that the A-l2s would gradually be placed in storage, with the process to be completed by the end of January 1968. In May 1967, Vance, stated that that SR·71s would assume responsibility for Cuban overflights by 1 July 1967 and would also have responsibility for overflights of Southeast Asia by 1 December 1967. Until these capabilities were developed, the A-12 was to remain able to conduct assignments on a 15-day notice for Southeast Asia and a seven-day notice for Cuba. All these arrangements were made before the A-12 had conducted a single operational mission. In the months that followed the initiation of operations in Asia, the A-12 demonstrated its exceptional technical capabilities. Soon some high-level Presidential advisers and Congressional leaders began to question the decision to phase out the A-12, and the issue was reopened.

The SR-71 was used by the Air Force until 1998. A total of 32 aircraft were built, 12 were lost in accidents, but none to enemy fire. Like the A-12, the SR-71 was designed for flight at over Mach 3 with a flight crew of two in tandem cockpits, with the pilot in the forward cockpit and the Reconnaissance Systems Officer (RSO) monitoring the surveillance systems and equipment from the behind cockpit. Again, like the A-12, the SR-71 was designed to have the smallest possible radar cross section. Finished aircraft were then painted a dark blue, almost black, to increase the emission of internal heat and to act as camouflage against the night sky. The dark colour also led to the aircraft's call sign of, "Blackbird". The SR-71 used the same J58 engines as the A-12 and had similar performance characteristics. The extra 6000kg weight of the SR-71 meant it could not fly quite as high as the A-12 with a ceiling of 85,000 feet compared to the A-12s 95,000 feet. The A-12 was also 0.5 Mach faster, but had a shorter range of 2200 nautical miles compared to the SR-71s 2900 nautical mile range. The first flight of the SR-71 took place on 22 December 1964, at Air Force Plant 42 in Palmdale, California.

The SR-71 was to have reported to have reached a top speed of Mach 3.4 during flight testing. The first SR-71 to enter service was delivered to the 4200th (later, 9th) Strategic Reconnaissance Wing at Beale Air Force Base, California, in January 1966.

SR-71s first arrived at the 9th SRW's Operating Location at Kadena on 8 March 1968, taking over from the A-12s. These deployments were code named GLOWING HEAT, while the program was code named SENIOR CROWN. North Vietnam reconnaissance missions over were code named GIANT SCALE. On 21 March 1968, Major Jerome F. O'Malley and Major Edward D. Payne flew the first operational SR-71 sortie in SR-71 from Kadena AB, Okinawa. From the start, SR-71 reconnaissance missions over enemy territory of North Vietnam, Laos, and others in 1968, was averaging at one a week for nearly two years. By 1970, the SR-71s were averaging two sorties per week, and by 1972, they were flying nearly one sortie every day. Two SR-71s were lost during these missions, one in 1970 and the second aircraft in 1972, both due to mechanical malfunctions. Like the A-12 though, the SR-71 was an expensive aircraft to run. Satellite technology had moved forward at an alarming rate and the need for the SR-71 grew less and less. The U-2 had found its niche and cost was a big factor in keeping it flying. The SR-71 was originally retired in October 1989, so money could be diverted to B-1 Lancer and B-2 Spirit programs. On 24 September 1994, congress voted to allocate $100 million for reactivation of three SR-71s. The SR-71 then continued to fly until October 1999 and the SR-71s final retirement. The SR-71 is still the fastest and highest flying production aircraft in the world. The only aircraft that was faster was the X-15, which could reach speeds of over 4,000 mph. The only aircraft ever to come close to the SR-71's speed besides the X-15 was the Russian MiG-25 Foxbat. The MiG-25 could only reach speeds of over Mach 3 for a few minutes though. The Anglo-French Concorde was the only aircraft besides the SR-71 that could fly at supersonic speeds for hours at a time. For the moment, the SR-71 is still the pinnacle of aircraft performance. One day in the future with emerging technologies and reduced costs, there may well be a successor to the SR-71, although I suspect that is likely to be unmanned.

SPECIFICATIONS

U-2

Crew: One
Length: 63 ft (19.2 m)
Wingspan: 103 ft (31.4 m)
Height: 16 ft (4.88 m)
Wing area: 1,000 ft² (92.9 m²)
Aspect ratio: 10.6
Empty weight: 14,300 lb (6,760 kg)
Max. takeoff weight: 40,000 lb (18,100 kg)
Powerplant: 1 × General Electric F118-101 turbofan, 19,000 lbf (85 kN)
Performance
Maximum speed: 434 knots (500 mph, 805 km/h)
Cruise speed: 373 knots (429 mph, 690 km/h)
Range: 5,566 nmi (6,405 mi, 10,300 km)
Service ceiling: 70,000+ ft (21,300+ m)
Flight endurance: 12 hours

A-12

Crew: 1 (2 for trainer variant)
Length: 101.6 ft (30.97 m)
Wingspan: 55.62 ft (16.95 m)
Height: 18.45 ft (5.62 m)
Wing area: 1,795 ft² (170 m²)
Empty weight: 54,600 lb (24,800 kg)
Loaded weight: 124,600 lb (56,500 kg)
Powerplant: 2 × Pratt & Whitney J58-1 afterburning turbojets, 32,500 lbf (144 kN) each
Payload: 2,500 lb (1,100 kg) of reconnaissance sensors
Performance
Maximum speed: Mach 3.35 (2,210 mph, 3,560 km/h) at 75,000 ft (23,000 m)
Range: 2,200 nmi (2,500 mi, 4,000 km)

Service ceiling: 95,000 ft (29,000 m)
Rate of climb: 11,800 ft/min (60 m/s)
Wing loading: 65 lb/ft² (320 kg/m²)
Thrust/weight: 0.56

YF-12
Crew: 2
Length: 101 ft 8 in (30.97 m)
Wingspan: 55 ft 7 in (16.95 m)
Height: 18 ft 6 in (5.64 m)
Wing area: 1,795 ft² (167 m²)
Empty weight: 60,730 lb (27,604 kg)
Loaded weight: 124,000 lb (56,200 kg[6])
Max. takeoff weight: 140,000 lb (63,504 kg)
Powerplant: 2 × Pratt & Whitney J58/JTD11D-20A high-bypass-ratio turbojet with afterburner
Dry thrust: 20,500 lbf (91.2 kN) each
Thrust with afterburner: 31,500 lbf (140 kN) each
Performance
Maximum speed: Mach 3.35 (2,275 mph, 3,661 km/h[6]) at 80,000 ft (24,400 m)
Range: 3,000 mi (4,800 km)
Service ceiling: 90,000 ft (27,400 m)
Armament
Missiles: 3× Hughes AIM-47A air-to-air missiles located internally in fuselage bays
Avionics
Hughes AN/ASG-18 look-down/shoot-down fire control radar

SR-71
Crew: 2 (Pilot and Reconnaissance Systems Officer)
Payload: 3,500 lb (1,600 kg) of sensors
Length: 107 ft 5 in (32.74 m)
Wingspan: 55 ft 7 in (16.94 m)

Height: 18 ft 6 in (5.64 m)

Wing area: 1,800 ft2 (170 m2)

Empty weight: 67,500 lb (30,600 kg)

Loaded weight: 152,000 lb (69,000 kg)

Max. takeoff weight: 172,000 lb (78,000 kg)

Powerplant: 2 × Pratt & Whitney J58-1 continuous-bleed afterburning turbojets, 34,000 lbf (151 kN) each

Wheel track: 16 ft 8 in (5.08 m)

Wheelbase: 37 ft 10 in (11.53 m)

Aspect ratio: 1.7

Performance

Maximum speed: Mach 3.3[89][90][N 5] (2,200+ mph, 3,540+ km/h, 1,910+ knots) at 80,000 ft (24,000 m)

Range: 2,900 nmi (5,400 km)

Ferry range: 3,200 nmi (5,925 km)

Service ceiling: 85,000 ft (25,900 m)

Rate of climb: 197 ft/s (60 m/s)

Wing loading: 84 lb/ft^2 (410 kg/m^2)

Thrust/weight: 0.44

Printed in Great Britain
by Amazon

23642667R00046